"Theologically grounded a clear direction to any church that desires to be welcoming and accessible to people with disabilities and their families. I'm grateful for Sandra Peoples's advocacy on behalf of families like mine and creating ways for all people to experience God's plans, purposes, and blessings through disability."

Laura Wifler, mom to a child with a disability; author, *Like Me: A Story About Disability and Discovering God's Image in Every Person*

"Sandra Peoples has provided a biblically grounded and clinically aware guide to disability ministry. As the dad of a young adult with autism, I was moved by the compassion and intentionality expressed in *Accessible Church*. As a church leader, I'm grateful for a resource that's practical and scalable for congregations of different sizes and budgets. This will be my go-to recommendation for churches looking to start or mature a ministry to special-needs children, students, adults, and their families."

Jared Kennedy, Managing Editor for Books and Curriculum, The Gospel Coalition; author, *The Beginner's Gospel Story Bible* and *Keeping Your Children's Ministry on Mission*

"Few churches are equipped to welcome our brothers and sisters with disabilities, not because we don't want to but because we don't know how. Sandra Peoples wants to help churches be well prepared for the task. Her pioneering work is a gift to the church. If you are a pastor who desires to serve saints with disabilities, you and your staff need this book."

Daniel Darling, Director, The Land Center for Cultural Engagement; author, *The Dignity Revolution* and *Agents of Grace*

"Sandra Peoples has given us a plethora of practical steps in this important book. Her many years of living with people with disabilities and working 'in the trenches' has produced wisdom that she translates effectively into pragmatic, down-to-earth models for ministry in the church. The church needs to read, absorb, and apply this wisdom. I am grateful Sandra has labored long to produce this faithful resource, and I recommend it heartily and with gratitude."

Michael S. Beates, Chaplain and Bible Teacher, The Geneva School; author, *Disability and the Gospel*

"As a father of a son with a disability, I've seen firsthand the profound beauty and challenges that come with raising a child who doesn't fit the world's narrow definition of 'normal.' But Sandra Peoples reminds us in *Accessible Church* that God's grace shines brightest in our weakness. This book is a powerful call to the church to embrace families like mine—not with pity but with purpose. People with disabilities are not to be looked down on; they are some of the greatest teachers of God's goodness, joy, and unconditional love. Sandra weaves together theology, personal experience, and practical wisdom to show how every church can be a place where the gospel reaches and transforms everyone. This is more than a book; it's an invitation to see God's glory in unexpected places."

Shane Pruitt, National Next Gen Director, North American Mission Board; author, *9 Common Lies Christians Believe*

"In my estimation, this is the most complete book on disability ministry that is currently available. Sandra Peoples approaches a bevy of crucial topics with biblical wisdom, ministerial understanding, practical knowledge, and personal experience. This is more than a book; it is a valuable resource, and a necessary tool, for anyone who has come alongside individuals whose lives are impacted by disability."

Chris Hulshof, Disability Ministry Program Director, John W. Rawlings School of Divinity at Liberty University; author, *Jesus and Disability: A Guide to Creating an Inclusive Church*

"Every church should be accessible to everyone. In *Accessible Church*, Sandra Peoples casts a compelling vision of the *why* and *how* of becoming more accessible to the disabled community. Read this book, but more importantly, do whatever it takes to implement the wisdom it contains."

Kyle Idleman, Senior Pastor, Southeast Christian Church, Louisville, Kentucky

Accessible Church

Accessible Church

A Gospel-Centered Vision for Including People
with Disabilities and Their Families

Sandra Peoples

Foreword by Joni Eareckson Tada

WHEATON, ILLINOIS

Accessible Church: A Gospel-Centered Vision for Including People with Disabilities and Their Families

© 2025 by Sandra Peoples

Published by Crossway
   1300 Crescent Street
   Wheaton, Illinois 60187

Cover design: David Fassett

First printing 2025

Printed in the United States of America

Trade paperback ISBN: 978-1-4335-9818-0
ePub ISBN: 978-1-4335-9820-3
PDF ISBN: 978-1-4335-9819-7

Library of Congress Cataloging-in-Publication Data

Names: Peoples, Sandra, author.

Title: Accessible church : a gospel-centered vision for including people with disabilities and their families / Sandra Peoples ; foreword by Joni Eareckson Tada.

Description: Wheaton, Illinois : Crossway, 2025. | Includes bibliographical references and indexes.

Identifiers: LCCN 2024045077 (print) | LCCN 2024045078 (ebook) | ISBN 9781433598180 (trade paperback) | ISBN 9781433598197 (pdf) | ISBN 9781433598203 (epub)

Subjects: LCSH: Church work with people with disabilities. | People with disabilities—Services for. | Disabilities—Religious aspects.

Classification: LCC BV4460 .P46 2025 (print) | LCC BV4460 (ebook) | DDC 259/.4—dc23/eng/20250108

LC record available at https://lccn.loc.gov/2024045077

LC ebook record available at https://lccn.loc.gov/2024045078

Crossway is a publishing ministry of Good News Publishers.

VP   34 33 32 31 30 29 28 27 26 25
15 14 13 12 11 10 9 8 7 6 5 4 3 2 1

Thank you to the churches who have welcomed my entire family because they were accessible to my sister Syble and my son James:

First Baptist Church, Duncan, Oklahoma
Stewartstown Baptist Church, Stewartstown, Pennsylvania
Heights Baptist Church, Alvin, Texas

Contents

Foreword

NEARLY EVERY CUL-DE-SAC in America includes a family that deals with disability. Life is anything but easy for them. Nonstop disability routines, butting heads with the school system, meltdowns, cleanups, insurance hassles, therapy appointments, lack of respite—all this sets the stage for isolation and depression.

To be fair, there are some disabling conditions that are easy to manage. But there are always bone-weary parents who must lock the doors and windows at night to keep their hyperactive child with autism from escaping.

These homes need the gospel to walk through their front door. They need Jesus in the flesh to enter their world. Yet, God is doing everything from his end. He is fully engaged and at work to give peace and strength to parents and comfort to bewildered kids. He is fighting, his Holy Spirit is warring on the side of his families where a disabling condition has snuffed out hope.

And God has called you to fight alongside him. As a volunteer or staff worker in disability ministry, you embody the good news where the bad news feels overwhelming due to disability. You speak words of hope; you become the gospel, wooing special needs families who otherwise would never come to church.

You create welcoming spaces, networks of support and friendship, access to biblical teaching, counseling, and worship. You help shape your church into a home that embraces every family member, regardless of disability. You fight, advocate, love, pray, and rejoice when families affected by disability find their place in the body of Christ.

Sandra Peoples has done all this and more. She is one of the most respected "go-to" guides when it comes to disability ministry. She grew up alongside a sister with Down syndrome and raised a son with level 3 autism. She understands the need, has advocated for change, has loved on hurting families, prayed for the impossible, and watched her congregation joyously become what church should be: a body of weak and needy people all leaning hard on Jesus.

Sandra has now poured all her insights and best practices into the remarkable book you hold in your hands. *Accessible Church* is not merely an instruction book on how to set up a special-needs department. It's more personal than that. As my advocate-friend Jackie Mills-Fernald often says, some churches are content to have you serve at a safe, arm's-length distance, untouched and unscathed within neat and tidy programs. But as a disability ministry worker, you don't do a program—you do a person.

Finally, Sandra Peoples takes you deep into the theological context for embracing families that live with disability. This is because disability ministry reminds the church of something it has forgotten, and that is that we are all frail, enfeebled, and in need of God's transforming grace. Ministry to special-needs families forbids the gospel to be conveyed from a position of power; rather, it requires that we all enter Christ's kingdom from a point of grace. For aren't we all needy in God's eyes? Isn't this why the "weaker [members] are indispensable" (1 Cor. 12:22)?

I applaud Sandra's work in *Accessible Church*. Her book will help you win the heart of your church for disability ministry. Not a special-needs department or something segregated and separated off to the side. Rather, you will bring the church back to its roots as it integrates special-needs families into the fold. Your congregation will then not only be giving the gospel but embodying it. Not only declaring the good news but becoming truly great news to families who need Christ desperately.

Great work, Sandra!

Joni Eareckson Tada
JONI AND FRIENDS INTERNATIONAL
DISABILITY CENTER

Author's Note about Terminology

I AM THANKFUL FOR self-advocates who help family members and ministry leaders understand how the language used to describe them makes them feel. In writing and editing, I have considered current preferences and the most widely used terminology. I understand that in the future use of this book, acceptable language may further evolve, and I ask for your understanding that our intent is to honor and respect, never offend.

Introduction

I WAS BORN into a church-going family. Members of my family had attended First Baptist Church in Duncan, Oklahoma, since it was founded. My great grandparents' house was right behind the church, and they often hosted the pastor and his family for Sunday lunch. My great grandmother played the organ there for years. In the next generation, my grandmother served as the preschool director, and my grandfather was an usher in the balcony. Kids would climb the stairs to see him each Sunday because when they shook his hand, he slipped them a Tootsie Roll.

I was also born into a disability family. I grew up with a sister with Down syndrome. That diagnosis, which came shortly after her birth just days after Christmas in 1977, could have changed our church involvement. It meant her development wouldn't be the same as her peers'. She would need extra time to do the crafts, extra explanations to understand the lesson, and extra eyes on her because she could be pretty mischievous—like getting into the snacks before snack time or heading down the hall to find Grandpa and his pocket full of candy. Would the church where my family had served for decades be able to serve our family by being accessible to Syble and therefore our entire family?

For many churches, the answer isn't an automatic yes. The extras that people with disabilities may need at church can feel like too much, and many churches think they have already reached their limits. There are no extras—no extra time to learn, no extra cash in the budget, no extra volunteers to serve, and no extra room to put people with disabilities.

There's a story in the Gospels of a group of people who have also reached their limits. And like what often happens in churches today when they feel like they've reached their limits, a person with disabilities suffers. A paralytic man is cut off from accessing Jesus and from the people who followed Jesus. But in Mark 2, the group finds ways to overcome their limitations! Verses 1–3 say, "And when [Jesus] returned to Capernaum after some days, it was reported that he was at home. And many were gathered together, so that there was no more room, not even at the door. And he was preaching the word to them. And they came, bringing to him a paralytic carried by four men."

These four men want to bring their friend to Jesus. They have likely heard of his reputation as a healer. And hearing that Jesus is in a home, they see an opportunity to bring their friend close to him. At this time, people with disabilities were blocked from having access to the temple. According to New Testament scholar Craig Keener, teachings from the *Mishnah Hagigah* and other Jewish documents would have prevented those who were lame and blind from entering the temple.[1]

By being cut off from the temple, people with disabilities were also cut off from the community built around the rhythms related

---

1   Craig S. Keener, *The Gospel of Matthew: A Socio-Rhetorical Commentary* (Eerdmans, 2009), 502. For a discussion on the topic, see also Chris H. Hulshof, *Jesus and Disability: A Guide to Creating an Inclusive Church* (B&H, 2022), 46.

to worship, sacrifices, and feasts. No temple and no community. This paralytic man is in a desperate situation—a situation made worse by his inability to save himself. But his friends have hope. They just have to find a way in. Mark continues, "And when they could not get near him because of the crowd, they removed the roof above him, and when they had made an opening, they let down the bed on which the paralytic lay" (2:4).

They have similar challenges to the ones we face today: no time (Jesus may only be passing through and there for a short time), no volunteers (It's up to just the four friends), and no space (They can't even open the door). But instead of seeing these as hindrances they can't overcome, the friends use them as motivation. I can almost hear their optimism: "There's no time like the present! We can do it together! We can't get through the door, but we can make a way through the roof!" It makes me smile just to think of it. Maybe these men are young. I can see my teenage son coming up with a plan like this with his friends much more easily than I can picture my husband and his middle-aged friends with their fully formed prefrontal cortexes and bad backs!

The men in this biblical story overcome their challenges and find a way to get their friend to the healer they have heard about, but Jesus's reaction may have surprised them: "And when Jesus saw their faith, he said to the paralytic, 'Son, your sins are forgiven'" (2:5). Your sins are forgiven! Is that what they came for? Did they know Jesus believed he could forgive sins? It certainly surprises some in the crowd:

> Now some of the scribes were sitting there, questioning in their hearts, "Why does this man speak like that? He is blaspheming!

Who can forgive sins but God alone?" And immediately Jesus, perceiving in his spirit that they thus questioned within themselves, said to them, "Why do you question these things in your hearts? Which is easier, to say to the paralytic, 'Your sins are forgiven,' or to say, 'Rise, take up your bed and walk'? But that you may know that the Son of Man has authority on earth to forgive sins"—he said to the paralytic—"I say to you, rise, pick up your bed, and go home." (2:6–11)

Jesus perceives their thoughts and responds to them with a question: "Which is easier, to say to the paralytic, 'Your sins are forgiven,' or to say, 'Rise, take up your bed and walk'?" (2:9).

How would you respond to the question of which is harder, to forgive sins or heal a man who could not walk? Some believe it's easier to say, "Your sins are forgiven," because there's no observable proof of your success or failure. You can't see sins being forgiven. You can see whether a man who came in on a mat through a hole in the roof walks home without assistance. But the audience at this time would have known it's much harder to say you can forgive sins. Being able to forgive sins is something only God himself can do. It's a serious claim to make, and one that eventually leads to Jesus's crucifixion. John 5:18 says, "This was why the Jews were seeking all the more to kill him, because . . . he was even calling God his own Father, making himself equal with God."

With these words, Jesus is showing his authority over both sin and sickness to this audience in Capernaum. He is making a claim only he can make and prove. "And [the paralytic man] rose and immediately picked up his bed and went out before them all, so that they were all amazed and glorified God, saying, 'We never saw anything like this!' " (Mark 2:12). When we encounter Jesus, we are amazed, and we glorify God. And that experience should motivate us to bring others to him, no matter what obstacles seem to stand in our way.

Just like the paralytic man who could not save himself, not even take a step toward Jesus on his own, we come to Jesus in the same state of desperation. None of the work we do to try to overcome our sin can release the hold it has on us. That is, until it is met with the power of Jesus. Paul tells us in Ephesians how those who are dead in sin become alive again in Christ:

> But God, being rich in mercy, because of the great love with which he loved us, even when we were dead in our trespasses, made us alive together with Christ—by grace you have been saved—and raised us up with him and seated us with him in the heavenly places in Christ Jesus, so that in the coming ages he might show the immeasurable riches of his grace in kindness toward us in Christ Jesus. (Eph. 2:4–7)

Like the paralytic man, we are forgiven and raised up. This is the good news of the gospel, and this message is at the heart of everything else you will read in this book. We modify lessons, provide noise-reducing headphones, and give support to those who are dysregulated so they can hear and have an opportunity to respond to the gospel. The goal is the gospel—you'll read those words again and again on the pages to come.

We can see from the story of these four friends that we aren't the first to face the idea of accessibility and be overwhelmed by our own limitations. But we aren't bound by those limitations because when it comes to reaching people with the gospel, God has shown himself faithful over and over to overcome those limitations and call people to himself.

Our church welcomed Syble and made accommodations for her from birth until our family moved away when she was nineteen. And because they made room for her, my whole family was able to attend together. I heard the gospel in that church. I was baptized there. And while sitting in those pews as a teenager, I prayed that God would use me in ministry. Experiencing what Jesus did in my life drives me to make that relationship possible for every single family, especially families like mine, whose lives have been radically altered by a diagnosis from a doctor or therapist.

In this book, we will walk together through each step. I'll introduce you to people who've been working in this space for decades—people with disabilities, caregiving families, pastors and ministry leaders—who will guide us. We'll empower you to be like the paralytic man's four friends: to overcome obstacles and bring more people to Jesus. I can't imagine a more exciting opportunity. We'll be amazed by what God will do, and we'll glorify him together. Are you ready to help your church become an accessible church?

1

Laying the Foundation

A Theology of Disability

IF YOU READ ONLY ONE BOOK about disability ministry, I don't want it to be this one. If you're going to read just one book about God's design and purpose for people with disabilities, how he expects his followers to treat people with disabilities, and the lengths he will take to ensure they are welcome in his family and his church, it shouldn't be this one. Because all that and more is in Scripture. If you're going to read just one book about inclusion and accessibility, it should be the Bible.

The theme of disability crops up all through the Bible, from Genesis to Revelation. The commentary *The Bible and Disability* lists almost two thousand verses and passages on disability.[1] In *Disability and the Gospel*, Michael Beates focuses on thirty-nine. If you read through the Bible in a year like I did this year, you'll

---

1   Sarah J. Melcher, Mikeal C. Parsons, and Amos Young, eds., *The Bible and Disability: A Commentary* (Baylor University Press, 2017).

see the passages pop up in the narrative.[2] Jacob limps and leans on his staff. Moses tells God he can't speak before Pharaoh because he is slow of speech. Mephibosheth, the lame son of Jonathan, is invited to King David's table. Paul writes of a thorn he asked God to remove, which may have been a chronic condition that affected his eyesight.

Throughout this book, we'll see how passages on disability set the framework for why and how we do disability ministry. The Bible isn't a disability ministry handbook, but it's a head and heart book—it teaches us how to think about disabilities and how to treat those with disabilities (including how to view ourselves if we are ever diagnosed with a disability).

To begin, let's focus on passages that illustrate the overarching view of disabilities in Scripture. We will build our theology of disability on these passages. Jen Wilkin and J. T. English write in their book, *You Are a Theologian*, that theology is a means of organizing the ideas given to us in God's word. So when I talk about building a theology of disability, what I mean is organizing and understanding passages in Scripture about disability. Having a theology of disability matters because, as they write, "we think differently, feel differently, and act differently as a result of developing better categories for understanding God."[3]

In our disability ministry world, we sometimes put theologians and practitioners in different categories: Theologians *think* about disability and the Bible, and practitioners *do* disability ministry.

---

2   Robert Smith, ESV Chronological Reading Plan, *ESV* podcast, https://www.crossway .org/.

3   Jen Wilkin and J. T. English, *You Are a Theologian: An Invitation to Know and Love God Well* (B&H, 2023), 19.

But we are all theologians, and developing our theology of disability makes us better practitioners. You are a theologian, and you have a theology of disability. Let's make sure that theology has a firm foundation that will hold up when we are ministering to people with disabilities and their families. To do that, we're going to look at God's *plan*, God's *purpose*, God's *provision*, and God's *promise* in disability.

God's Plan

We will start at the beginning of the world as we build our theology of disability. It starts with our theology of man, which of course begins at creation:

> Then God said, "Let us make man in our image, after our likeness. And let them have dominion over the fish of the sea and over the birds of the heavens and over the livestock and over all the earth and over every creeping thing that creeps on the earth."
>
> So God created man in his own image,
>   in the image of God he created him;
>   male and female he created them. (Gen. 1:26–27)

Man was created by God and in the image of God. Being created in the image of God sets humans apart from everything else God created. However, the fall and sin distort our ability to reflect God perfectly, but the image of God remains in each person.

What it means to be created in the image of God has been discussed for centuries and has not always been agreed on. Theologians Joel Beeke and Paul Smalley remind us, "As fallen human beings, we are not in a position to understand the image of God completely. We do not fully know what it means to be human."[4] Even though we can't fully know, what we do understand about the image of God has implications for how we view and treat others, especially those with disabilities.

Beeke and Smalley underscore that "the image consists centrally of inward righteousness and a right relationship to God, but more broadly encompasses man's whole nature along with his divinely ordained function."[5] What's helpful about this view is that it doesn't reduce God's image to only the roles we play or the capacities we have.

Although the image of God can include functions and characteristics, it is more than that. If the image of God were only about our dominion over the earth, those who have opportunities to have more dominion might be seen as reflecting more of God's image. Or if it were primarily about intelligence and understanding, those with the highest IQs would resemble God most. Instead, 1 Corinthians says, "But God chose what is foolish in the world to shame the wise; God chose what is weak in the world to shame the strong . . . so that no human being might boast in the presence of God" (1:27, 29). If it were only about doing, would we still image God if we failed to function? Instead of only imaging God (a verb), we are the image of God (a noun). The image is about who man is and not just what he does.

Beyond being simply functional, the image of God is also relational. Being able to have a relationship with God and having

---

4 Joel R. Beeke and Paul M. Smalley, *Reformed Systematic Theology*, vol. 2, *Man and Christ* (Crossway, 2020), 204.

5 Beeke and Smalley, *Man and Christ*, 193.

the potential for salvation and sanctification (the ability to reflect Jesus, who *is* the image of God) is an essential characteristic of the *imago Dei*. It is holistic and ontological, based on who people are and not what they do. John Kilner writes, "Being made in the image of God involves connection and reflection. Creation in God's image entails a special connection with God and also God's intention that people be a meaningful reflection of God, to God's glory."[6] This understanding better represents realities for people with disabilities who reflect the image of God. As John Hammett contends, "We may affirm that each person has the capacity for a relationship with God because we believe God has the capacity to reach every human spirit."[7]

As Beeke and Smalley remind us, we won't fully know what Scripture means by "image" and "likeness" in Genesis 1, but we know enough to treat all people with respect and dignity and to understand all people have the potential to have a relationship with God. This matters in our evangelism to and our discipleship of people with disabilities. Seeing all people as image bearers is the reason we need to do disability ministry. We can see everyone as God sees them, with the potential of having a relationship with him and with others. Colossians 1:16 says, "All things were created through him and for him." Through him and by him we were created, and he created us for himself—for his plan and his praise. In our diversity, even in the diversity of our physical abilities and disabilities, social

6 John F. Kilner, *Dignity and Destiny: Humanity in the Image of God* (Eerdmans, 2015), 311.

7 John S. Hammett, "Human Nature," in *A Theology for the Church*, rev. ed., ed. Daniel L. Akin (B&H, 2014), 320.

strengths and deficits, and intellectual challenges and achievements, we ourselves are evidence of his love and care for each one of us.

In Psalm 139, David writes of this love and care in God's creation of himself. In the sensory class I teach each week at our church, the Seeds Kids Worship version of this Psalm is the first song I play. I want our kids to know that God has a plan for their design, and that his plan is for their good and his glory. They can echo what David knows to be true:

> For you formed my inward parts;
> you knitted me together in my mother's womb.
> I praise you, for I am fearfully and wonderfully made.
> Wonderful are your works;
> my soul knows it very well.
> My frame was not hidden from you,
> when I was being made in secret,
> intricately woven in the depths of the earth.
> Your eyes saw my unformed substance;
> in your book were written, every one of them,
> the days that were formed for me,
> when as yet there was none of them. (139:13–16)

Disabilities are diagnosed at different times in a person's life. My sister Syble's Down syndrome was written into her DNA in our mother's womb. My son James's autism wasn't detectable until the gaps between his development and the development of other kids his age became too clear to ignore. Joni Eareckson Tada had a diving accident at age seventeen that left her a quadriplegic. These verses in Psalm 139 make it clear that no matter when a diagnosis comes, it is under the sovereign plan of God.

God's Purpose

Ephesians 2:10 says, "For we are his workmanship, created in Christ Jesus for good works, which God prepared beforehand, that we should walk in them." Each one of us is his workmanship. We are clay in the hands of a loving potter (Isa. 64:8). Being born with a disability or developing one later in life is not a sign of faithlessness or weakness on our part or a mistake or anger on God's part. Disabilities may be results of the fall, but they are still part of God's plan and his purpose for our lives.

Exodus 3–4 records a conversation between Moses and God that is foundational to our understanding of disabilities and God's sovereignty. God reveals himself to Moses through a burning bush and tells him about his expectations for Moses's advocacy and leadership for his people. Moses has many excuses for why he can't fulfill this calling. In 4:10–12, Moses even tries to use his limitations as an excuse: "But Moses said to the LORD, 'Oh, my Lord, I am not eloquent, either in the past or since you have spoken to your servant, but I am slow of speech and of tongue.' Then the LORD said to him, 'Who has made man's mouth? Who makes him mute, or deaf, or seeing, or blind? Is it not I, the LORD? Now therefore go, and I will be with your mouth and teach you what you shall speak.'" What's profound about this response is that it's clear—and clear in such an early account for the followers of God—that God takes credit for disabilities.

There is no guessing, no assuming, no excusing. God says, "Is it not I" who is fully responsible for your creation? As Michael Beates writes,

> We have discovered that God is not only creator of man and we are made *imago Dei*, but we have seen that God is declared to be the creator of disabilities. He is also, in some profound sense, the source of brokenness and the one who has ordained to use such brokenness for his purposes, and ultimately, for his glory.[8]

"How could this be?," you may ask. How could something that leads to suffering and hardships be part of God's plan? We all wrestle with this question. When my son James was diagnosed with autism, I questioned what God's purpose would be in his life and the life of our family. I had grown up with a sister with Down syndrome, so I knew firsthand some of the barriers we would encounter. On his first day of special-education preschool, I locked myself in the bathroom and cried as I called out to God. "Why James? Why us?" If there was a lesson he was trying to teach me, I considered this to be a cruel way to teach it.

In that moment (and in every moment since then), I've had to hold on to what I know is true about God when I'm struggling to bring my emotions in line with his truths. *God loves me. God loves James*, I repeated that day in the bathroom. I repeated it when we were adjusting his medications, and he was reacting with self-injurious meltdowns he couldn't control. *God loves me.*

God loves James. I repeated it when we celebrated his sixteenth birthday with Blue's Clues decorations and a new swing set instead of keys to a car like his big brother had gotten. *God loves me. God loves James.*

Eareckson Tada writes, "God permits what he hates to accomplish that which he loves."[9] And that which he loves—his purpose—can be seen in the life of James and others who have disabilities. We see it in another of the best-known passages about disabilities, John 9:1–3: "As he passed by, he saw a man blind from birth. And his disciples asked him, 'Rabbi, who sinned, this man or his parents, that he was born blind?' Jesus answered, 'It was not that this man sinned, or his parents, but that the works of God might be displayed in him.'"

As I was adjusting to having a son with a diagnosis and all that would mean for our family, this passage brought me peace and hope. But now as I look at it from the broader perspective of a ministry leader, I see the context it was written in and the application not only for the family of the man born blind but also for those of us caring for special needs families.

First, let's think about the purpose for this miracle and the other miracles of Jesus. Jesus heals many people, but he doesn't heal everyone. Some people he heals show evidence of their faith before the healing, and some after. Some are healed by a touch, whereas others have to take steps to receive healing. Some show appreciation for their healing, while others do not. For some, Jesus heals them and also says their sins are forgiven, as we saw in Mark 2 with the paralytic man. What is consistent in each healing

---

9   Joni Eareckson Tada, *Pearls of Great Price: 366 Daily Devotional Readings* (Zondervan, 2006), Dec. 12.

miracle recorded is the healer. Jesus heals to show his power over sickness, suffering, and death. Albert Wolters writes, "Christ's work was not only a preaching of the long-awaited coming of the kingdom, but also a *demonstration* of that coming. In his words, and especially in his deeds, Jesus himself was proof that the kingdom had arrived."[10]

Jesus's healings do more than restore sight or mobility or health. They also restore relationships and communities. As Lamar Hardwick observes, "An examination of [Jesus's] healing ministry strongly suggests that the central theme and aim of his healing ministry was to restore people who were disabled and disregarded back into the community."[11] This restoration of connection is seen in his healings and teachings (in Luke 14 and Matt. 21 specifically).

Second, let's place this encounter with the man born blind into the wider scope of John's Gospel. Professor Chris Hulshof connects it to Jesus saying "I am the light of the world" in John 8 and to his good shepherd discourse in John 10. Without these important connections, we might wrongly assume that this man glorified God only after his healing. Instead, as Hulshof writes, "God was glorified through the visual validation that Jesus Christ is the Messiah and his representative. Thus, the focus is shifted from the blind man and directed to both God the Father and God the Son."[12]

---

10 Albert M. Wolters, *Creation Regained: Biblical Basis for a Reformational Worldview*, 2nd ed. (Eerdmans, 2005), 74 (emphasis original).

11 Lamar Hardwick, *Disability and the Church: A Vision for Diversity and Inclusion* (InterVarsity Press, 2021), 52.

12 Chris H. Hulshof, *Jesus and Disability: A Guide to Creating an Inclusive Church* (B&H, 2022), 126–27.

The connection to Jesus's teaching on what it looks like to be a good shepherd comes from the reactions of those in the life of the man who was born blind. His neighbors, the Pharisees, and even his parents discuss his condition out of curiosity, not care. Jesus calls himself the good shepherd and gives examples of what it looks like to be a good shepherd. But in the story with the man born blind, the people (and specifically the religious leaders) do not exhibit these characteristics. Again from Hulshof: "For Jesus, leaders who lack the divine compassion and sympathy for the blind man give evidence that they are not true shepherds. Further, the inability of these leaders to recognize this divine compassion and mercy in Jesus only adds to their indictment."[13]

Seeing God's purpose in creating people with disabilities in Exodus 4 and noticing Jesus's purpose in healing people with disabilities helps provide guardrails for our own thinking about disabilities. They are not accidental or without purpose. They are not a result of our sin or God's apathy. In my own experience after receiving my son's autism diagnosis, I was able to read James 1:17 through this lens: "Every good gift and every perfect gift is from above, coming down from the Father of lights." If my son's autism was from God, then somehow it must be a good and perfect gift for the purpose of making us more like Christ and to bring others to him. It is part of his purpose for us.

God's Provision

We can see that God takes responsibility for disabilities and has a purpose for them. We can also see that God provides for the

---

13   Hulshof, *Jesus and Disability*, 121.

disabled. This truth is seen most clearly in the stories of David's practical provision for Mephibosheth and God's sufficient grace for Paul.

Consider the former:

David asked, "Is there anyone remaining from the family of Saul I can show kindness to for Jonathan's sake?" There was a servant of Saul's family named Ziba. . . .

So the king asked, "Is there anyone left of Saul's family that I can show the kindness of God to?"

Ziba said to the king, "There is still Jonathan's son who was injured in both feet."

The king asked him, "Where is he?"

Ziba answered the king, "You'll find him in Lo-debar. . . . So King David had him brought from the house of Machir son of Ammiel in Lo-debar.

Mephibosheth son of Jonathan son of Saul came to David, fell facedown, and paid homage. David said, "Mephibosheth!"

"I am your servant," he replied.

"Don't be afraid," David said to him, "since I intend to show you kindness for the sake of your father Jonathan. I will restore to you all your grandfather Saul's fields, and you will always eat meals at my table."

Mephibosheth paid homage and said, "What is your servant that you take an interest in a dead dog like me?"

Then the king summoned Saul's attendant Ziba and said to him . . . "Mephibosheth, your master's grandson, is always to eat at my table." . . .

. . . Mephibosheth lived in Jerusalem because he always ate at the king's table. His feet had been injured. (2 Sam. 9:1–10, 13, CSB)

After many military victories, David experienced a season of peace. Scripture says he "administered justice and equity to all his people" (2 Sam. 8:15). It was at this time that David thought of his friend Jonathan and wanted to show kindness to any surviving relatives. He found out there was a survivor—Mephibosheth. Earlier, in 2 Samuel 4:4, we read this about him: "Saul's son Jonathan had a son whose feet were crippled. He was five years old when the report about Saul and Jonathan came from Jezreel. His nanny picked him up and fled, but as she was hurrying to flee, he fell and became lame. His name was Mephibosheth" (CSB).

Mephibosheth was now a man and was summoned to approach the king who was ultimately responsible for the death of his father and grandfather. The very king who in his anger at being mocked by the Jebusites (who said even their blind and lame could hold David off) had made a law that the blind and lame couldn't live within the city of Jerusalem (2 Sam. 5:6–8). Mephibosheth fell at David's feet in fear as he was brought before the king. But David responded with restoration, invitation, and compensation. David restored to him the land of Saul and Jonathan, three miles north of Jerusalem in Gibeah. He extended an invitation to sit at his table, and "so Mephibosheth ate at David's table just like one of the king's sons" (2 Sam. 9:11, CSB). David also offered compensation, giving to him "all that belonged to Saul and . . . his house" (9:9). Mephibosheth then lived in Jerusalem and "ate always at the king's table" (9:13).

Functional and Social Aspects of Disability

There are two aspects of disability: *functional* and *social*. The functional aspect of disability is the impairment itself. For example, my son with autism is functionally nonverbal. He can speak fewer than one hundred words. The social aspect of disability is the treatment of the disabled person by society. Because James can speak so few words, people don't speak to him, even to ask a question he might be able to answer. His limited language is a barrier, and so is the assumption by others that he won't be able to communicate.

The current postmodern worldview trend is to focus on only social aspects of disability and downplay or deny functional aspects. In this view, the only barriers are those created and enforced by society. This worldview presents functional aspects not as debilitating but simply as differences that are neither good nor bad.

The biblical worldview of disabilities acknowledges both the functional and social realities. Addressing the functional aspects, we can say that bodies and brains don't function as they should, as they would have before the fall. Addressing the social aspects, we can say that society has created barriers that make it harder for people with disabilities to flourish. In our churches, we can focus on decreasing the social barriers that exist for people with disabilities.

God's provision for Mephibosheth is clear in these verses. Mephibosheth was at the mercy of David: He fell on his face before him, calling himself a servant to David and "a dead dog." In humility and with fear, he came when David summoned him. But instead of finding wrath because of the actions of his grandfather, he was met with grace. It is important to note that Mephibosheth doesn't receive an invitation to the table after he is healed. He remains lame. God's provision doesn't equal healing. It does equal his grace.

The thorn Paul speaks of in 2 Corinthians 12:7–10 is also evidence of this grace:

> So to keep me from becoming conceited because of the surpassing greatness of the revelations, a thorn was given me in the flesh, a messenger of Satan to harass me, to keep me from becoming conceited. Three times I pleaded with the Lord about this, that it should leave me. But he said to me, "My grace is sufficient for you, for my power is made perfect in weakness." Therefore I will boast all the more gladly of my weaknesses, so that the power of Christ may rest upon me. For the sake of Christ, then, I am content with weaknesses, insults, hardships, persecutions, and calamities. For when I am weak, then I am strong.

In 2 Samuel, David is a representative of God's grace in the life of Mephibosheth. In Paul's epistle, he also experiences God's grace, even though his suffering is not alleviated. Instead of growing bitter and resentful, Paul grows in Christlikeness as he identifies with Christ in his sufferings and finds strength. We are all broken, needy people. People with disabilities just can't hide their neediness as easily as the rest of us try to hide ours. But in that neediness we find God's sufficiency—his provision. As Jesus says in John 15:5, "I am the vine; you are the branches. Whoever abides in me and I in him, he it is that bears much fruit, for apart from me you can do nothing."

God's Promise

The final piece to building our theology of disability is looking at God's promise to all of us. I quoted from Beeke and Smalley at the beginning of the chapter, and the rest of that quote helps us now: "We do not fully know what it means to be human. But we will know. . . . One day the image will be revealed to those who belong to Jesus Christ and—beyond all dreams and expectations—we will share in it."[14] As Paul writes in 1 Corinthians 15:49, "Just as we have borne the image of the man of dust, we shall also bear the image of the man of heaven."

Being made in the image of God is mysterious to us now, and so is understanding exactly what our eternities will look like in heaven. We do know there will be an end to the suffering we experience here on earth—both the functional and social aspects of disability will pass away. Revelation 21:4 says, "He will wipe away every tear from their eyes, and death shall be no more, neither shall there be mourning, nor crying, nor pain anymore, for the former things have passed away." Thomas Boehm helps us apply this verse to experiences with disability: "God's promise is to swallow up death and wipe away tears from our faces. As this

14 Beeke and Smalley, *Man and Christ*, 204.

glorious truth relates to disability, whatever brings us loss, sorrow or discomfort in this life will no longer have the power to do so—whether that source be the functional impairment associated with disability, the socially-induced aspects of disability, or some combination of both."[15]

This healing in heaven includes far more than people with disabilities looking, acting, feeling, moving, communicating, and thinking like people without disabilities. The healing we will receive is that all of us will be more like Christ. As 1 Corinthians 15:51 says, "We shall not all sleep, but we shall all be changed." Our reproach will be taken away (Isa. 25:8). We will spend eternity without hindrances to our fellowship with each other or our worship of God. Anything about us now that holds us back from fellowship and worship will be no more. That promise makes me long for heaven, where I will be able to have a conversation with my son for the first time and where we will praise God side by side.

In all we can imagine about heaven, especially as those who have disabilities or love people with disabilities, Eareckson Tada helps us focus on what's most important:

When I was first injured, I only viewed heaven as a place where I could get back what I had lost. I would receive hands that worked and feet that walked and even danced. For me, it wasn't 'the Day of Christ,' it would be 'the Day of Joni.' My attitude changed as I studied the Scriptures. I realized that heaven was mainly focused on Jesus, not me . . . I also began to understand that every fringe benefit of heaven—whether receiving my new

---

15 Thomas Boehm, "10 Pillars of a Theology of Disability," Wheaton Center for Faith and Disability, www.wheaton.edu/faithanddisability.

body, a new home, new friends, whatever—really centered around the culmination of Christ's purposes and his kingdom.[16]

As we look at all Scripture, from Genesis to Revelation, we can trust in God's plan, purpose, provision, and promise for those with disabilities. This foundation will set us up for how we include those who are affected by disabilities and their families in our churches.

Bringing It All Together

Based on what you learned in this chapter, here are steps of accessibility you can take:

Start by seeing yourself as a disability theologian.

Then try choosing two or three passages listed in this chapter and dig deeper into understanding their context and application.

Next, apply what you've learned to cast a biblical vision for including people with disabilities at your church.

---

16 Eareckson Tada, *Pearls of Great Price*, April 13.

2

Who Is Missing?

Do Our Pews Reflect Our Communities?

ACCORDING TO A LIFEWAY RESEARCH study done in 2020, "Nearly every pastor (99 percent) and churchgoer (97 percent) says someone with a disability would feel welcomed and included at their church."[1] When special needs families saw that survey result, they felt a disconnect between what these pastors believe is true about their churches and what they had personally experienced. A closer look at the data reveals what pastors said their churches actually do to make people with disabilities feel welcome:

- Three in four pastors say their church encourages congregants to volunteer in community events (like Special Olympics) for people with disabilities.

---

1 "Churches Believe They Are Welcoming to Those With Disabilities," Lifeway Research, March 10, 2020, https://research.lifeway.com/.

- Most say their church gives financial assistance to families with ongoing needs (70 percent) or provides respite for family caregivers to give them a break (60 percent).
- Half of churches provide an additional teacher to aid a person with special needs in a class.
- Nearly a third (29 percent) of pastors say their church provides classes or events specifically for people with disabilities.[2]

The study went to on to reveal that "larger churches are more likely than others to say they help in many of these specific ways."[3] The biggest gap was seen in the percentage of churches that say they offer classes or aides for people with disabilities. While 75 percent of churches with worship attendance topping 250 say they provide such assistance, as do 54 percent of churches with 100 to 249, 46 percent of churches with 50 to 99, and 35 percent of churches with fewer than 50.[4]

Although some of the self-reported stats are encouraging, there is still a large number of the population who want to attend church but are unable to because churches near them aren't taking steps to be accommodating. According to the 2000 census, nearly one in five families in the United States has a member with a disability.[5] We can also look at school data for the number of children in our cities who have disabilities. According to the National Center for Education Statistics, in the 2022–2023 school year, 15 percent of

2 "Churches Believe They Are Welcoming to Those With Disabilities."
3 "Churches Believe They Are Welcoming to Those With Disabilities."
4 "Churches Believe They Are Welcoming to Those With Disabilities."
5 "Nearly 1 in 5 People Have a Disability in the U.S., Census Bureau Reports," United State Census Bureau, July 25, 2012, https://www.census.gov/newsroom/releases /archives/miscellaneous/cb12-134.html.

total public-school students (ages three to twenty-one) received special education services under the Individuals with Disabilities Education Act.[6] Add in students with learning disabilities and mental health or behavior diagnoses who fall under 504 accommodations (which come from Section 504 of the 1973 Rehabilitation Act), and you're likely close to 20 percent in your school district.[7] I reached out to an administrator in my school district (a suburb of Houston, Texas), and she said 18.78 percent of the students in our district have an IEP (individualized education program) plan and 7.83 percent have a 504 plan. That's 26.61 total, or 1 in 4.

Most of us aren't seeing this percentage of the population represented in our worship centers. They are missing from our children's ministry classrooms, our youth group activities, and our adult small groups. But in Luke 14, Jesus makes it clear where they would be represented when he shared the parable of the great banquet:

> So the servant came back and reported these things to his master. Then in anger, the master of the house told his servant, "Go out quickly into the streets and alleys of the city, and bring in here the poor, maimed, blind, and lame."
>
> "Master," the servant said, "what you ordered has been done, and there's still room." (Luke 14:21–22, CSB)

6 "Students with Disabilities: How Many Students with Disabilities Receive Services?" National Center for Educational Statistics, US Department of Education, https://nces.ed.gov/fastfacts/display.asp?id=64.

7 Laurie U. deBettencourt, "Understanding the Differences between IDEA and Section 504," *Teaching Exceptional Children* 34 (Jan/Feb 2002), available at https://www.cmcss.net/wp-content/uploads/2021/06/Understanding-the-Differences-between-IDEA-and-Section-504.pdf. See also "Profile of Students with Disabilities in the U.S. Public Schools During the 2020–21 School Year," US Department of Education, February 2024, available at https://www.ed.gov/media/document/crdc-student-disabilities-snapshotpdf.

Jesus uses this parable to teach his audience what the kingdom of God will look like. In Luke 14, he is eating at the house of a ruler of the Pharisees (14:1). In response to noticing how they chose places of honor at this dinner (14:7), Jesus tells the parable of the wedding feast and the parable of the great banquet. These parables would have taught the Pharisees how the kingdom of God would not meet their expectations. First Jesus says, "For everyone who exalts themselves will be humbled" (14:11, CSB), and then he gives them a picture of what heaven will look like that includes "the poor and crippled and blind and lame" (14:21).

Today we can look around our churches to see who may be missing, just like the master saw who was missing from his banquet. Michael Beates asks in his book, *Disability and the Gospel*,

Do these kinds of people today feel welcome at God's banquet in the church? Too often, sadly they do not. Too often, merely coming to church is too much of a burden. People encounter both physical and social obstacles. And how many churches intentionally go about the business of seeking such people and using the church's manpower to go and bring them in? Again, too often, the church does not.[8]

But we can learn from Jesus just as his audience at the time did. Maybe you look at your ministries and think, *There isn't room here for kids with extra needs.* Considering the list of limits we talked about in the introduction, maybe you're already low on space, low on volunteers, and low on money, and the idea of this

8 Michael S. Beates, *Disability and the Gospel: How God Uses Our Brokenness to Display His Grace* (Crossway, 2012), 54.

kind of new ministry feels intimidating because of all the unknowns. Thankfully, Jesus already addressed that concern. Because the servant told the master, "Sir, what you have commanded has been done, and still there is room," we can trust that when we invite people with disabilities into our churches and into fellowship with us, it does not take away from those who are already present. Lamar Hardwick, a pastor who is autistic, writes,

> Apprehension about creating disability-inclusive churches is to be expected, but the cost should not be the cause for ignoring the calling to include the disabled. Jesus has personally assured us that when we set the table and send the invitation to the disabled first, God will be responsible for the results and the reimbursement.[9]

Based on the percentages from recent census stats and special education data, we can see many of our churches are not reaching this portion of the population.

Who Is Missing?

What families are we talking about when we look around for who is missing? They include people in three categories: those with physical and cognitive disabilities (sometimes referred to as special needs), learning disabilities, and mental health conditions. Or, like we say at our church, "Anyone who needs modifications to the way we present the message or to the environment in order to be able to hear, understand, and respond to the gospel." Let's

---

9   Lamar Hardwick, *Disability and the Church: A Vision for Diversity and Inclusion* (InterVarsity, 2021), 46.

break down each category and look at the number of people they represent in our communities.

Disabilities

When most people think of special needs ministry, they picture people with physical and cognitive disabilities. My family falls into this category—having a sister with Down syndrome and a son with level 3 autism and intellectual disabilities. Every day of my life I've been in a special needs family, first as a sister and then as a mom. I can speak to the challenges of these roles, and I can tell you they would be impossible for me to face without the hope of the gospel. Which is why I want every sibling, parent, and person with a disability to have a church family like the one I grew up in and the one that welcomes me now. That is possible only when churches also welcome my sister and my son.

Special-needs diagnoses can come at different times, depending on the diagnosis. My parents got my sister's diagnosis minutes after her birth. My son got his diagnosis soon after his third birthday. Most of the diagnoses we're talking about in this category happen in the preschool years, from birth to five. Learning disabilities and behavioral diagnoses often come in the elementary years, and mental health diagnoses can come at any stage. But a person can become part of the disability community at any age—for example, after a car accident that leaves someone paralyzed, or when receiving a diagnosis such as Alzheimer's. In chapter 6 we will discuss how to support a family when they receive a diagnosis and the stages of grief and resilience it will go through, but first we will focus on what is considered a special-needs diagnosis.

When we're talking about ministry participants with special needs or disabilities, we're talking about these diagnoses:

- Down syndrome: This is a chromosomal abnormality that affects 1 in 700 babies in the US and includes physical markers and cognitive delays.[10]
- Cerebral palsy: This is the most common motor disability in childhood and affects 1 in 345 children.[11]
- Deaf or hard of hearing: 2 to 3 in every 1,000 children in the US have a detectable level of hearing loss in one or both ears at birth.[12]
- Blind or low vision: Nearly 3 percent of children younger than 18 are blind or visually impaired, the latter being defined as struggling to see even with glasses or contacts.[13]
- Rare diseases and disorders: One example is Angelman syndrome, which affects 1 in 12,000 to 20,000 people in the general population, according to National Organization for Rare Disorders.[14]
- Autism: This is the biggest diagnosis in this category, with numbers being updated often. In 2020, 1 in 36 children

10 "Down Syndrome," Center for Disease Control, May 16, 2024, https://www.cdc.gov/.
11 "Cerebral Palsy," Cerebral Palsy Guide, https://www.cerebralpalsyguide.com/.
12 Centers for Disease Control and Prevention (CDC), "Identifying Infants with Hearing Loss: United States, 1999–2007," *Morbidity and Mortality Weekly Report* 59, no. 8:220–23.
13 "Fast Facts: Vision Loss," Centers for Disease Control and Prevention (CDC), May 15, 2024, https://www.cdc.gov/.
14 "Angelman Syndrome," National Organization for Rare Disorders, updated February 14, 2018, https://rarediseases.org/.

aged 8 had been diagnosed with autism.[15] According to the most recent *Diagnostic and Statistical Manual of Mental Disorders* definition, there are three levels of autism: level 1, which requires minimal help to complete daily tasks (previously referred to as Asperger's); level 2, which requires moderate help; and level 3, which requires significant help.[16]

Many of these families with these diagnoses aren't attending church because the barriers are too hard to overcome, including wondering whether they'd even feel welcomed. For example, a 2018 study found children with autism are 84 percent less likely to attend church than their typical peers.[17] As we learned, approximately 1 in 36 children in the US aged 8 years old are on the autism spectrum, so that's a significant number of students we aren't seeing on Sunday mornings. To reach families with special needs and disabilities, churches must be proactive to be welcoming and accessible.

Learning Disabilities

When my son David was young, I saw signs of dyslexia as he struggled with reading, spelling, and handwriting. Since I home-

---

15 Matthew J. Maenner et al., "Prevalence and Characteristics of Autism Spectrum Disorder Among Children Aged 8 Years—Autism and Developmental Disabilities Monitoring Network, 11 Sites, United States, 2020," *Surveillance Summaries* 72, no. 21 (March 24, 2023), available at https://www.cdc.gov/.

16 *Diagnostic and Statistical Manual of Mental Disorders* (DSM-5), American Psychiatric Association (APA), 2013.

17 Andrew L. Whitehead, "Religion and Disability: Variation in Religious Service Attendance Rates for Children with Chronic Health Conditions," *Journal for the Scientific Study of Religion* 57, no. 2 (June 2018): 377–395.

schooled him, we were able to take it slowly and use lots of resources designed for kids with learning disabilities. He didn't even realize how far behind he was without peers to compare himself to or bad grades coming home in his backpack each week. The only place he felt embarrassed and "dumb" was at church.

The children at our church at the time did a Scripture memory program on Wednesday nights. David and I worked together on the assigned verses each week, but there was still lots of academic-type work to do when they met together at church. David's friend was a strong reader and would often help him pronounce words or spell them correctly, but the teacher of the class didn't have much patience for David's struggles. One week in front of everyone, he told David he needed to go to real school to learn to read because he was so far behind. That teacher was stern with David anytime he made a mistake, to the point that David made more mistakes and developed anxiety over attending. Even now as a teenager, David can remember how it felt to be singled out and made to feel small due to learning differences he can't control.

Churches aren't academic settings, but there are often academic-type expectations and activities during small group and Sunday school times. This is when we will see children with learning disabilities struggle, often through their behavior. Learning disabilities are invisible disabilities, unable to be seen. And although many of us are familiar with dyslexia and some qualities of it, we may not know all the types of learning disabilities our students may have. The Learning Disabilities Association of America shares this list:[18]

18 "Learning Disabilities," Learning Disabilities Association of America, https://lda america.org/.

- Dyscalculia: This "affects a person's ability to understand numbers and learn math facts."[19]
- Dysgraphia: This "affects a person's handwriting ability and fine motor skills."[20]
- Dyslexia: This "affects reading and related language-based processing skills."[21]
- Non-Verbal Learning Disabilities: This "affects the ability to read nonverbal cues like facial expressions or body language."[22]
- Oral and Written Language Disorder and Specific Reading Comprehension Deficit: This "affects an individual's understanding of what they read or of spoken language. The ability to express oneself with oral language may also be impacted."[23]

There are also related disorders that affect learning for those who have been diagnosed:

- ADHD: This affects a person's ability "to stay focused and pay attention and can contribute to controlling behavior and hyperactivity."[24] This is also considered a mental health disorder.

19 "Dyscalculia," Learning Disabilities Association of America, https://ldaamerica.org/.
20 "Dysgraphia," Learning Disabilities Association of America, https://ldaamerica.org/.
21 "Dyslexia," Learning Disabilities Association of America, https://ldaamerica.org/disabilities/dyslexia/.
22 "Non-Verbal Learning Disabilities," Learning Disabilities of America, https://ldaamerica.org/.
23 "Oral / Written Language Disorder and Specific Reading Comprehension Deficit," Learning Disabilities of America, https://ldaamerica.org/.
24 "Attention-Deficit/Hyperactivity Disorder: What You Need to Know," National Institute of Mental Health, https://www.nimh.nih.gov/.

- Dyspraxia: This affects "movement and coordination, language, and speech." This is prevalent in people with cerebral palsy and other disabilities.[25]
- Executive Functioning: This "affects planning, organization, strategizing, attention to details and managing time and space." This is a quality in those with other disabilities, including autism.[26]

Mental Health and Behavioral Diagnoses

Mental health and behavioral diagnoses are also invisible disabilities that significantly affect a family's ability to be part of a church. Steve Grcevich, a child and adolescent psychiatrist, observes,

> I began routinely asking parents of the kids I was treating—kids with common conditions, including ADHD, anxiety, autism, depression, and other mood disorders—how their child's condition impacted their ability to attend church. Their answers made my jaw drop. I was struck by the hurt and disappointment described by parents following unsuccessful attempts to attend church together as a family.[27]

According to the CDC, "Mental disorders among children are described as serious changes in the way children typically learn, behave, or handle their emotions, which cause distress

---

25 "Dyspraxia," Learning Disabilities Association of Washington, https://ldawa.org/.

26 "Executive Functioning," Learning Disabilities Association of Washington, https://ldawa.org/.

27 Stephen Grcevich, *Mental Health and the Church: A Ministry Handbook for Including Children and Adults with ADHD, Anxiety, Mood Disorders, and Other Common Mental Health Conditions* (Zondervan, 2018), 17.

and problems getting through the day." They list these diagnoses as being common in children: anxiety, depression, Oppositional Defiant Disorder (ODD), Conduct Disorder (CD), ADHD, Tourette's syndrome, OCD, and PTSD.[28]

Traditionally, churches have not done well supporting those with mental health conditions, whether they are children, teens, or adults. But more and more people are understanding how brains and bodies suffer as a result of the fall. And regardless of the causes of mental health challenges, these families need the hope that the gospel provides and the care of a church family. We have the opportunity to show compassion and hospitality to those who struggle. That can start in our children's and youth ministry areas and grow to change the culture of the entire church for the better. As Ed Welch reminds us, "Emotional suffering needs spiritual encouragement."[29]

Adopted Children with Disabilities or Trauma

Over the years, churches have rightly encouraged their families to adopt, following the biblical mandate to care for those without families. But many churches are unprepared to support these families when the child the family adopted has a special-needs diagnosis. One study showed that 39 percent of adopted children have special health-care needs and 26 percent have moderate-to-severe health difficulties, compared to 19 percent and 10 percent in the general population.[30]

---

28 "Children's Mental Health Disorders," Centers for Disease Control and Prevention, https://www.cdc.gov/.

29 Edward T. Welch, *Side by Side: Walking with Others in Wisdom and Love* (Crossway, 2015), 26.

30 Sharon Vandivere, Karin Malm, Child Trends, and Laura Radel, "Adoption USA: A Chartbook Based on the 2007 National Survey of Adoptive Parents," Assistant Secretary for Planning and Evaluation, October 31, 2009, http://aspe.hhs.gov/.

My friend Tiffany's family adopted a child from a dissolution (in which the first adoptive family is unable to meet a child's needs and a second family adopts him). Their church, where her husband served on staff, didn't care for them postadoption as well as they could have. Tiffany shares,

> The children's ministry staff insisted that Elliot belonged in Sunday school and mid-week children's classes with children of his same age, but at ten years old he struggled to read, could not maintain self-control in a classroom environment, wiggled and fidgeted constantly, failed to keep his hands to himself, possessed no inside voice at all, and had an attention span more akin to that of a four-year-old. Overemphasis on school-like learning objectives meant that the classes were inaccessible to him in every way, but leadership doggedly refused to allow him to attend a more developmentally appropriate class.

The traditional ministry structure did not work for Tiffany's son, who has been institutionalized, traumatized and neglected, twice adopted, malnourished, and delayed.

By taking steps to be more accessible to special-needs families, we can make sure these orphans who are now sons and daughters have the support of their church families as well.

A Model of Belonging

Now that we understand who may be missing from our church families, let's talk about the shift in culture that will happen at our churches when we become more accessible. That shift will require vulnerability on the part of both the church and the disability family. As churches, we may need to lay down our preferences, our traditions, and our reputations for the sake of the gospel. Near the end of his earthly life, Jesus gave us an example of what our priorities should be.

After his triumphal entry reported in Matthew 21, Jesus cleansed the temple:

> And Jesus entered the temple and drove out all who sold and bought in the temple, and he overturned the tables of the money-changers and the seats of those who sold pigeons. He said to them, "It is written, 'My house shall be called a house of prayer,' but you make it a den of robbers." And the blind and the lame came to him in the temple, and he healed them. (21:12–14)

The money-changers and those selling pigeons were likely set up in the area designated for Gentiles and those who were ritually unclean, including people with disabilities. They were blocked from access to the temple and from fellowshiping with those who were permitted to enter. Jesus overturned the tables, and as a result "the blind and the lame came to him in the temple, and he healed them" (21:14). Jesus removed them so those with disabilities could come close to him in the temple.

We can also break down barriers and invite those without access to come close to Jesus and be part of our church families. Amy Fenton Lee writes,

> We as the church do not want to lag behind society today, in terms of welcoming people of differing cultures, races, and abilities. Practically, this plays out many ways—thinking about others and

our differences when we design ministry space, produce videos for the worship center, select praise songs, and develop curriculum. It's the church's responsibility to thoughtfully, intentionally, and respectfully engage everyone—because God loves them all. That's the gospel being lived out for all to see and experience.[31]

To do that, we can apply what Stephanie Hubach calls the model of belonging. In this model, as laid out in her book *Same Lake, Different Boat*, each party is required to enter the life of the other in a way that brings blessing to everyone.[32] The person with a disability and the church body both humble themselves for the benefit of the other. Asking for help isn't easy. Appearing weak isn't rewarded by our society. Answering with anything other than "I'm fine!" on a Sunday morning takes humility and trust. Those with disabilities often can't hide their dependence on others. But they can communicate those needs in a way that invites the church to respond with kindness and an openness to consider the requests. Ed Welch reminds us, "We take initiative and move toward each other. God has moved toward us; we move toward others in his name."[33]

Hubach explains the steps we need to take to move toward each other in humility:

Person A's request for accommodations can be made in a way that communicates desire or need (both of which embrace

---

31 Amy Fenton Lee, *Leading a Special Needs Ministry: A Practical Guide to Including Children and Loving Families* (B&H, 2013), 48.

32 Stephanie O. Hubach, *Same Lake, Different Boat: Coming Alongside People Touched by Disability*, rev. ed. (P&R, 2020).

33 Welch, *Side by Side*, 73.

vulnerability) *or* in a way that is rights-oriented or demanding (both of which avoid vulnerability). In a parallel fashion, B can respond in a way that welcomes, listens, and adapts (embracing vulnerability) *or* in way that ignores, rejects, and self-protects (avoiding vulnerability).[34]

So we, empowered by the Holy Spirit, can offer hope and hospitality to the person requesting accommodations.

But what if person A, the special-needs family, doesn't approach a church with vulnerability? Are we off the hook? Stephanie answers this question: "While both parties are responsible for their actions, the onus is on the church—as the body of Christ— to initiate and pursue welcoming and belonging even if the needs of person A are great and their approach is less than desirable."[35] With this in mind, we move forward in vulnerability, focusing less on "them" and "us" and more on mutual flourishing for the goal of every family having access to the gospel message and gospel-centered community.

Being an accessible church benefits the church as well as the families who are included. Many of our church members have told us how much they enjoy seeing our son James and the friends in his class worship together during our services. Others have grown in empathy and understanding about the challenges that people with disabilities and their families face. One lady in the church told my husband that she saw a boy having a hard time at the grocery store one day. She saw that he was wearing noise-reducing headphones like James does, so she knew he likely was

---

34 Hubach, *Same Lake, Different Boat*, 24 (emphasis original).
35 Hubach, *Same Lake, Different Boat*, 245.

having a meltdown. She encouraged his mom with a smile and an offer to help. Members from other churches tell me stories like these when I visit their churches for trainings and consultations.

The anecdotal evidence that healthy churches are accessible churches led Jim Roden, lead Pastor of Journey Church in Tucson, Arizona, to do his doctoral dissertation on how church health's best-kept secret is being disability inclusive. Here is what he says about such inclusion: "When churches minister to them [people with disabilities] and with them and are open to receive from them, they [churches] are better for it, and their people grow spiritually."[36] Ryan Wolfe of Ability Ministry agrees that including people with disabilities can positively influence a church. He writes,

> When Disability Ministry is added to a local church in the right way it has the ability to both heal and grow that church in a way that no other ministry can. Why? Because people with disabilities are central to the heart of God and designed by God for belonging in the local church (Luke 14:21, 1 Cor. 12:22, John 9:3).[37]

Now that we understand better the size and scope of the mission field that exists in our communities, we can move toward people with disabilities and their families in vulnerability and make

---

36 Jim Roden, "DATC2023—Jim Roden—Church Health's Best Kept Secret: Inclusive Disability Ministry," Key Ministry, May 4, 2023, YouTube video, https://www.youtube .com/. This session was at the Disability and the Church Conference 2023, hosted by Key Ministry.

37 Ryan Wolfe, "Disability Ministry Is a Thermostat Ministry." Ability Ministry, December 9, 2022, https://abilityministry.com/.

accessibility modifications that will help them feel welcome at our churches so they can respond to the gospel. We have a foundation for *why*, and in the following chapters we will discover the *how*.

Bringing It All Together

Based on what you learned in this chapter, here are steps of accessibility you can take:

Start by learning about different disabilities and common lingo.

Then try inviting families in your church and community to meet and talk about their experiences and ask what they may need to be fully included.

Next, apply what you've learned by writing a mission statement for the ministry at your church.

3

Preparing for Accessibility

Programs, Places, and Policies

ONE SUNDAY MORNING, Elizabeth sat in a different spot than usual in the worship center. In front of her was a family she hadn't met before—a mom and a dad with two sons. The younger of the two sons sat between his parents. Well, he kinda sat. During the welcome, Scripture reading, opening prayer, and music, he wiggled in his chair, he laid on the floor, he used his chair as a spot to draw, he stood on his toes and rocked back and forth during the music while he covered his ears, and when it was time to sit down again to listen to the sermon, he tried to get past his dad and into the aisle. His family was prepared. His mom had a deep purse with drawing paper and colored pencils, chewing gum, and a spinner fidget toy. His dad anticipated the move for the aisle and blocked it. His older brother wasn't surprised by the movements of his brother or the attention he got.

Some of that attention came from the other church members around them when the younger son spoke to his parents at a distracting volume and couldn't get comfortable during the sermon. After a few minutes, the dad took his son out of the service. The mom and older son stayed through the sermon but left as soon as the congregation stood for the final song. Elizabeth slipped out behind them and saw the family reunite in the lobby, where the husband had watched the service on the TV screen while his son was entertained by his iPad. They seemed eager to get out of the doors before the lobby filled up with people at the end of the service, but Elizabeth approached them to introduce herself.

"Hi! I'm Elizabeth Jenkins. I'm so glad you guys came to church today! I was sitting behind you and realized we hadn't met yet."

The mom introduced herself as Jessica and then introduced her husband, Grant, and their sons, Zach and Levi. Levi continued to play on his iPad while his family chatted with Elizabeth.

"Levi has trouble sitting through church services," Jessica told Elizabeth. "He has autism and some sensory issues. We keep trying and sitting for as long as we can!"

"I have a nephew with autism who is a couple years older than Levi!" Elizabeth replied. "He has trouble sitting in the service for too long too, but our church came up with some great ideas for helping him participate and feel comfortable in the children's ministry and in the services. If you'll give me your number, I'll give it to our children's ministry director, and she can reach out this week to get to know you guys."

"That sounds great," Grant said as Elizabeth handed Jessica her phone so she could type in her number. "We've visited this church a few times, but we haven't met anyone because we are in and out so fast. We saw an announcement slide about an upcoming respite night for special-needs families, so we thought y'all might have something that would be a good fit for Levi on Sunday mornings too. We've just been so busy with school and therapy and Special Olympics; we haven't signed up or reached out."

Elizabeth replied that she understood how busy they were. She let them know she would pass on their info and that the children's ministry director, Shannon, would reach out soon. As Grant and Jessica Miller pulled out of the parking lot, they felt seen and understood. They had hope that this church might be a good fit for every member of their family.

Approach, Ask, and Adjust for Accessibility

Jessica and Grant's story is exactly what I want to happen at my church on a Sunday morning. Elizabeth took steps that I hope every member of my church would take if they sat behind a family like Levi's. In Scripture, we see Philip take steps of accessibility with the gospel message when he saw an Ethiopian eunuch seated in his chariot, reading from Scripture. The Ethiopian eunuch had a need (understanding what he was reading), and Philip was able to meet that need by taking three steps we can emulate: approach, ask, and adjust for accessibility.

Acts 8:26–28 sets the scene. An angel appeared to Philip and told him to go "south to the road that goes down from Jerusalem to Gaza":

> And there was an Ethiopian, a eunuch, a court official of
> Candace, queen of the Ethiopians, who was in charge of all

her treasure. He had come to Jerusalem to worship and was returning, seated in his chariot, and he was reading the prophet Isaiah. And the Spirit said to Philip, "Go over and join this chariot." So Philip ran to him and heard him reading Isaiah the prophet and asked, "Do you understand what you are reading?" And he said, "How can I, unless someone guides me?" And he invited Philip to come up and sit with him. . . . Then Philip opened his mouth, and beginning with this Scripture he told him the good news about Jesus (8:27–35).

In these verses, we see the three steps Philip took. Philip *approached the man* after the Holy Spirit prompted him. In fact, the verse says Philip ran! He was eager to meet this man and talk to him. When Philip heard him reading from the book of Isaiah, he *asked him a question*: "Do you understand what you are reading?" Philip could tell the man needed help. The court official had been to Jerusalem to worship and was reading from the Scriptures, but he didn't know the full story about Jesus. It was like he left before hearing the good part. So Philip *adjusted for accessibility* by starting at the beginning and sharing the good news about Jesus. The result: The Ethiopian eunuch understood the gospel message and asked to be baptized (8:37)!

In our churches, we can follow the same pattern with special-needs families. We approach them with kindness, we ask questions to figure out the challenges they're facing, and we adjust so they have the opportunity to understand and respond to the gospel. *Approach, ask, adjust for accessibility.* Just like Elizabeth after she sat behind Levi and his family. Just like Philip with the Ethiopian eunuch.

In the next few chapters, we're going to discuss how to set up a ministry that is inclusive and meets the diverse needs of children, teens, and adults with disabilities. When we approach special-needs families and ask how we can serve them, we'll be ready with options to adjust for accessibility. In this chapter we'll explore the places where this inclusion will happen, and in chapter 4 we'll think through who will be on the ministry team. Then in chapter 5 we'll learn how to best meet students' learning needs and support positive behavior. We'll follow along with the Miller family and the staff of the church they're visiting to see all the steps they take to prepare to welcome Grant, Jessica, Zach, and Levi.

What Is the Goal of Inclusion?

Let's start the practical part of this chapter with the goal of accessibility in churches. Our goal is the same goal that Philip had with the Ethiopian. Our goal is to share the good news about Jesus—the gospel. We want every person with a disability and their family to be able to hear, understand, and respond positively to the gospel. It may sound simple, but every decision you make about the placement of a child, how to adjust the curriculum for a teenager, and what outreach events you will offer should filter through this goal. It's the foundation for everything we do in disability ministry!

In addition to wanting their children to hear and respond to the gospel, parents tell us about the goals they have for their children at church. They are also simple—safety and belonging. They want their children to be safe, and they want them to build relationships with their peers, teachers, and mentors. These needs aren't different from the needs typical kids and teenagers have. In fact, they aren't different from the needs I have at church. I want to feel safe, and I want to feel like I belong.

Setting up the proper environment is the first step to meeting these goals. At our church, we say a person receives help from the disability ministry team if they need adjustments to the environment or to the lesson in order to hear and respond to the gospel. There are two parts to this inclusion: the environment and the lesson, or the classroom placement and the curriculum. Let's start by looking at the environment or classroom options.

Accessible Environments

There are four common options for accessible environments: inclusive, specialized, a hybrid of both, and reverse inclusion. The first three—inclusive, specialized, and a hybrid—are common in children's ministry. Reverse inclusion works well for teens and young adults. And for older adults with intellectual disabilities, a specialized environment can best meet their needs. In this chapter, chapter 4, and chapter 5, we will focus on children's ministry accessibility. In chapter 7, we'll focus more on ministry for and with teens and adults with disabilities.

Inclusive Environments

An inclusive environment is in the typical class with same-age peers, often with help from a teen or adult buddy who is specially trained to support the student. Many churches, especially small- to mid-sized churches, have only this type of ministry environment available. All the kids they serve are in the same classes. (In some of the church plants and newer churches I've visited, all the kids are in the same big room.) You can certainly make this work if it's your best or only option.

Inclusive environments are usually the best option for kids who have what we call invisible disabilities. These invisible or hidden disabilities include emotional, behavioral, and developmental disorders/diagnoses with no apparent physical symptoms or characteristics. They can include kids with ADHD, anxiety disorders, autism spectrum disorder (level 1), learning disabilities, and attachment disorders (common in adopted and foster care children).

According to child and adolescent psychiatrist Steve Grcevich, the families of children who have invisible disabilities are unique in their own ways. They don't always consider their kids to have disabilities or special needs. They consistently hear more bad news than good news. They feel discouraged and isolated. They are less likely to attend church than a typical family and are more likely to have had negative past experiences. The good news is these students can often be successful with a few changes. Serving the students well can make huge, positive changes for the entire family. For children with invisible disabilities, the ways we help them are often invisible as well.

Meeting the Challenges of Children with Invisible Disabilities

Children with invisible disabilities who are in our regular, inclusive classrooms face challenges we need to be aware of so we can best support them. Some of these challenges include:

- struggling with self-regulation and impulse control (such as throwing, hitting, and talking out)
- executive function deficits (following multiple directions)
- immature social skills
- verbal and nonverbal working memory deficits (remembering their Bible when they leave)
- feeling uneasy in the less-structured environment at church (compared to school)
- experiencing OCD-like behaviors
- sensory seeking or avoiding tendencies
- challenging social interactions
- experiencing rigid behaviors, inflexibility
- lacking empathy or being overwhelmed by the emotions of others
- preferring concrete language, which isn't always used at church ("Ask Jesus into your heart . . .")
- having specific areas of interests

There are changes we can make that benefit the kids who struggle and can benefit all our kids. We'll look at ideas for changes now, and in chapter 5 we'll see examples of these changes being used to support Levi when he attends Sunday school for the first time.

Classroom supports include how the class is structured and the sensory aids we can offer the kids. It's best for kids with disabilities to have a predictable routine week after week. That predictability lowers their anxiety and communicates safety. Teachers can post the schedule that the class will follow, and they can even use a visual schedule for those who struggle with reading. Knowing what to expect also decreases challenging behavior when it's time to transition from one activity to another (we often use the terms *preferred activity* and *nonpreferred activity*). A visual timer can also help with these transitions. For example, if the kids have a time of free play until quarter after nine and then will sit around the tables, you can post that on the visual schedule and at nine set the visual timer to count down fifteen minutes so the kids see how much time they have left to play. One reason I like using a visual timer is that I'm no longer the "bad guy" who makes them stop playing. The timer communicates it's time to stop and transition.

During your time together, it's also very helpful to have clear and uncomplicated expectations. I like the phrase "invitation and expectation" to help me remember how to communicate clearly. We tell the kids what they're going to do and what expectations we have for them during that time. If I have a five-year-old who really wants to keep playing with blocks while the rest of the class is sitting in a circle ready to hear the story, I can give him a clear invitation and expectation: "Jackson, the timer told us it's time to listen to the story. Come sit on the carpet square next to Shelby and sit crisscross to show me you're ready." Or for our older kids: "Our friend Lily is getting baptized in the service this morning! We're going to walk (not run) to the worship center and sit on the front two rows to watch. When the baptism is over and the worship team starts a song, we will come back to the classroom and have a snack while we watch our lesson video. Let's line up and get ready to walk down the hall." If you have kids who consistently struggle with transitions or the routine, you can create a "first . . . then" visual aid that just shows what's happening first and what's happening next (the visual representations can have Velcro dots on the back so they can be switched out depending on the activity).

The classroom environment can also be adjusted in ways that help our kids with sensory issues and other challenges. The goal is for the room to be engaging but not overwhelming. Kids with sensory processing disorder take in all sensory input at equal levels and have trouble picking out what is most important. For example, if the teacher is talking while background music is playing, the florescent lights are buzzing, and another class is yelling and laughing on the playground outside the windows, the student can hear all that input but may not be able to focus on the teacher's voice. We can limit the extra noise by offering noise-reducing headphones. Also, many kids can listen better if their hands are busy doing something else. You can offer fidgets to the kids who need them to focus better.

We can also make modifications to help kids with learning disabilities and those who aren't reading at grade level. Our goal is not to produce perfectly complete workbooks or activity sheets but to make students feel safe and cared for so they can hear the gospel. Adaptations can include offering word banks when they have to fill in blanks or listing the answers on a dry-erase board to help everyone. We can also let the children tell their buddies their answers verbally instead of having to write them out. And we can remember not to call on them to read out loud (even into their youth-group years).

When I'm recommending all these modifications to children's ministry leaders, it's usually at this point in the conversation that they'll ask how the typical kids in the classroom feel about the extra attention and toys or tools some of the kids are getting. First, most kids today are accustomed to classmates getting help at school. They have friends coming in and out for speech therapy or reading help. There may be a couple of desks in the room where kids go so they have fewer distractions when they take tests. So unlike previous generations, their classrooms at school are more accommodating to kids with various needs. If the kids are asking about fidgets and noise-reducing headphones, you can describe the different ways people learn and how these tools can help them, a lot like how glasses help people see. I even suggest letting everyone have a fidget for a week or two. The kids who need them will keep using them, and the kids who don't will quickly lose interest.

All these modifications can make a big difference for kids in our inclusive classrooms. In the next two chapters, we'll explore how to organize the supports you offer to students and how to communicate with your team what those supports are. Let's look next at the specialized classroom that meets needs in ways different from how the inclusive classroom can.

Specialized Environments

A specialized classroom best meets the needs of kids, teens, and adults who are most comfortable in an environment that can accommodate their sensory sensitivities and provide a lesson that meets their cognitive abilities. This can include kids with autism levels 2 and 3, intellectual disabilities, Down syndrome, those with minimal verbal skills, and more. When we welcome a family, we would be wise to ask the parents what kind of environment their child is in at school. If the child is in a self-contained or life-skills class, he or she will likely be most comfortable in either a specialized classroom or a hybrid of both the inclusive and specialized environments.

Most specialized environments are in a sensory room. The room has the equipment to meet kids' sensory needs to help regulate their bodies. These kids can be either sensory seekers, who crave input, or sensory avoiders, who avoid input. You can design your sensory rooms to meet the needs of both. Items commonly found in a sensory room include an indoor trampoline, a ball pit, and a swing. The sensory room in our church also has pillows with different textures, marble runs, blocks to build with, cars to race, and lots of puzzles and books. If one of our kids has a special interest—like exploring space—we'll get toys and books related to that topic.

The kids who are in this classroom full-time also have their lesson in this space. Remember, our goal is the gospel. We want all our kids, including the ones who may never be able to verbally express their beliefs, to hear the gospel and feel the love of Christ through the service and support of those in the classroom with them. There are gospel resources you can use for kids with intellectual disabilities to help them meet their potential for learning. Disability-specific curriculum like the Special Buddies option from Lifeway is great. There are also independent curriculum creators, like Awe and Wonder and The Adapted Word, you can use or supplement with. If you want the lessons to match the lessons that the other kids are doing in their classes, you can use material from the age or grade-level class that most closely matches the cognitive abilities of the kids in the class. For example, we often use the kindergarten level option because it's easy to read and the activity sheets can be done by our kids with some assistance.

Communicating the Word to Children Who Don't Communicate with Words

For children with little or no verbal ability, our time with them at church can look more like babysitting than an opportunity for evangelism and discipleship. And while it's good that we provide care for them while the rest of their family members are in their discipleship groups and the worship service, we need to remember that our goal is sharing the gospel with these children as well.

Because they are made in the image of God, these kids have the potential to have a relationship with their Creator. Even if they are unable to communicate what they understand about God and his love for them, we can show that love through our attentiveness to their needs and by speaking the gospel over them. To train the teachers at my church in this practice, I studied methods used for infants and toddlers. One option that has worked well for us is the Sure Foundation curriculum from Truth:78. It includes short phrases that we consistently speak over the children in our classroom, phrases like "God made everything" and "Jesus is my friend."

We may not be able to ask kids at this level what they know about God, but we do know that God is able to make himself known to them. Our role in their lives is to be faithful to share the gospel with them and pray for the Holy Spirit to work in their hearts.

A Hybrid of Inclusive and Specialized Options

Most of the kids in the ministry at my church take a hybrid approach for their support—they spend time in the inclusive classroom with their peers, and when they need to, they go to the specialized environment to either help meet their sensory needs or have an adapted lesson. (In chapter 5, Levi will spend time in both classes, so you can see what it would look like for him.)

If you don't have a room available to turn into a sensory room, you could create a sensory corner in a classroom or add sensory activities to the hallway. You could put up a tent with pillows to the side in an inclusive classroom where a kid can rest if she's shutting down. An additional option is to lay out gel tiles in the hallway and let kids jump from tile to tile or play "the floor is lava" when they have extra energy and are struggling to sit still. Get creative to meet the specific needs of the kids in your ministry!

Policies and Safety

Now that we've looked at the programs and places you'll create for kids with disabilities, let's consider some policies you may need to adjust or create in order to provide a safe environment for everyone. Some of these policies will cover worst-case scenarios. I don't want to discourage you from welcoming families because reading through these possible situations can feel scary. The best way to face an unknown scenario is to be prepared. It would be better to be prepared for these situations and not need to follow the plan you have in place than to not have a plan at all.

Good communication with your volunteers will ensure everyone is on the same page and feels prepared for a challenging situation. Good communication with the parents is also important. They are agreeing to the level of help you offer by leaving their kids in your care with the training you have and the staff you have available.

First, it's helpful to confirm that your insurance policy covers those with disabilities just like it does every other person on campus or at a church event. If a kid with a diagnosis hits another kid, the coverage and process for filing a claim, if necessary, are the same. If a teenager has a seizure, it's the same. You can review your policy or call your agent to talk through specific situations, but know that your policy doesn't discriminate coverage based on diagnosis or disability.

Toileting Policies

Many children with disabilities aren't potty-trained on the same schedule as typical kids. You may need to adjust your church's policy to meet their needs. For example, if your policy states that a child can't move from the toddler room to the preschool room until he or she is potty trained, you may need to make an exception for a child with Down syndrome who would benefit from being with her same-age peers, even though she hasn't reached that developmental milestone yet. There are some disabilities that require toileting help at every age. Your church can talk to the families affected and come up with a policy that works for everyone. Some churches text the parents any time a change is required. Other churches apply the same requirements they have for younger ages, like having two adults present. However, privacy can be an issue with multiple students in a room and limited helpers. You can screen off an area in your sensory room when needed and call in an extra helper. At our church, we often do diaper changes when the volunteers for the second service are arriving and the volunteers for the first service are still there so we have double the number of adults. If your church serves (or hopes to serve!) families of teenagers and adults, consider getting a universal-sized changing table to meet their needs.

High Medical Needs

Children, teens, and adults with high medical needs can require extra care to keep them safe. If your church serves a large population with extra medical needs, consider recruiting a volunteer who has nursing experience or hire a nurse. The disability ministry at Houston's First Baptist Church began by welcoming families of medically fragile children. For decades they have been able to continue to welcome these families by being appropriately staffed with nurses and others in health care. Parents and ministry leaders can talk through the care available and what the church is comfortable offering. These conversations and policies are also important to have before camp, vacation Bible school, and respite events. You may need a policy for administering prescription medicine that applies at these extra events.

If a ministry participant requires an aid for mobility or communication, there needs to be a plan for that device in an emergency situation (such as fire, tornado, or safety threat). For example, if you have a child who uses a wheelchair and she's out of her chair and playing in the ball pit during an emergency situation, what is the plan for her and the chair? Or what's the plan for a child who uses an iPad or similar device for communication? Discuss your plan with his or her parents so everyone is on the same page.

Security for Eloping Children

Eloping—running away to avoid a demand or sensory stimulation—is common in children with autism and other similar diagnoses. When possible, identify the trigger and make a plan to help. For example, provide noise-reducing headphones when the music is loud. It's also helpful for the team to communicate and decide on the minimum requirements for compliance when you have a child or teen who struggles to follow lots of instructions. For example, does the child have to sit in a chair, or can he stand in the back while remaining in the classroom? Kids who tend to avoid demands are more likely to follow instructions when they feel like they have some agency in making the decision and are therefore less likely to try to avoid the situation. If you have a seven-year-old who isn't lining up with the rest of the class, instead of telling him to get in line, you could ask if he wants to get behind his friend Jake or at the end of the line with Mrs. Robin. He feels like he has agency to make that decision instead of being forced, and you are happy with either option. (We'll talk more about positive-behavior support in chapter 5.)

Another way to decrease eloping opportunities is to set up as many barriers as possible and train everyone in the path. Can you close doors or install safety devices on the doors? If you have a greeter who opens the door to the main entrance or lobby, train the volunteer not to open the door for a child who is alone. That greeter might be the last obstacle between the child and the parking lot. Remember to review your policies for vacation Bible school and other outreach events when the kids will be in a different routine and you will have kids who don't regularly attend.

Safety in the Classroom

First, you need to have a procedure for how to report injuries that occur in your ministry classrooms. Accidents happen (for kids with and without disabilities!), like throwing a toy that hits another student or tripping on the playground. You can have a physical or digital incident report form available and a clear procedure for who fills out the form and when they should fill it out (ideally as soon as they can after the incident happens). Then decide on the steps for follow-up communication: the procedures for gathering more info if there are questions, talking to parents (both the parents of the child who was hurt and the child who caused the injury), and making a plan for the future if the situation can be avoided.

For children, teens, and adults who can be aggressive or self-injurious, there needs to be clear communication on steps that will be taken to keep everyone safe. To keep all the ministry participants at our church safe, we invited my friend Tiffany Crow, who is a board-certified behavior analyst to observe and help us develop a policy. We call it our room-clear plan. We use the plan when it is safer to keep an individual who is exhibiting harmful behavior in one place (the room) and to move the rest of the individuals out of said room.

For us, the criteria for a clearing a room is continuous physical aggression, behaviors so distracting that class cannot continue (e.g., loud vocalizations), concern for physical safety of other individuals, or concern for human decency (behaviors being exhibited should be observed by as few people as possible to maintain dignity; examples include nudity, self-injurious behavior, and obvious inappropriate self-touching).

Developing a Room-Clear Procedure

Here are the steps my church discussed when developing our room-clear procedure:

1. When criteria for a room clear is met, the teacher will instruct volunteers and students to clear the room by stating something like, "Let's go see another room." (The assisting adults and teen buddies in the room know what the trigger phase is and what steps to take next.)

2. Volunteers should know the room-clear procedures in order to implement them as quickly as possible.

3. The designated teacher will lead students out of the classroom in a calm manner. (If the student exhibiting escalated behavior is blocking the doorway, the teacher should move toward the student and encourage or guide the student to move to a different area of the room).

4. When students have cleared the room of concern, they should immediately engage in an alternative activity.

5. A second adult needs to move into the room with the primary teacher and the student exhibiting escalated behavior as soon as possible. This second adult should assist with the safety of the student(s) and teacher(s).

6. To deescalate the behavior, follow the plan that is specific to that child. Examples can include bringing up a favorite topic to discuss, offering a sensory-focused alternative (like jumping on the trampoline), or giving the child a sour candy (which can help with panic attacks).

7. When the behaviors are diminished, resume class as quickly as possible. Refrain from discussing behaviors in front of other students or in front of parents. Teachers and volunteers should debrief with the ministry leadership to determine whether they will be able to follow the procedures differently or better next time. Parents of the individual with escalated behavior should also be debriefed privately.

Even though we have this plan laid out, we haven't had to use it. We've been able to safely deescalate situations or get the participant who is struggling with aggression safely out of the room and into a room where he or she is safer (this has been our sensory room, and we move the kids in that room to the attached room, where they have their snack and lesson time). But we feel safer knowing that the plan is in place if we need it. And we review it with the teachers who have participants in their classes who may exhibit these behaviors (this includes our Wednesday night teachers and volunteers).

In addition to discussing a plan for these situations, you may want to consider getting additional training like Crisis

Prevention Institute's certification on deescalating situations and providing safe physical holds. You may also be able to talk to your school district and ask if people from your church can attend their trainings with special-education staff. Again, I don't want this section to scare you and keep you from welcoming families, but it is helpful to have a plan for stressful situations before they happen.

Sexual Abuse Prevention

You will also need to ensure that volunteers who work with kids, teens, and adults with disabilities follow a policy designed to prevent sexual abuse. People with disabilities are more likely to be abused or assaulted than those without disabilities, and measures to keep them safe must be enforced. Background checks should be required for all volunteers, and I recommend you use a training program like the one from MinistrySafe that focuses on sexual abuse prevention. Review your expectations and policies often.

Bringing It All Together

After reading this chapter, you hopefully have a good idea of the options for inclusion that you will want to offer, how to set up those environments, and what policies you need to adjust or create for the safety of your ministry participants.

Based on what you learned in this chapter, here are steps of accessibility you can take:

Start by deciding what model of inclusion is most needed at your church based on your current needs.

Then try adjusting your current policies to be more inclusive. *Next, apply* what you've learned by adjusting the environments where inclusion will take place (in the typical classes or in a specialized sensory space).

4

Your Ministry Team

Everyone Has a Role in Accessibility

PASTOR NATHAN wrapped up the staff meeting by asking if anyone had met the visiting family he noticed in the service that week. "It looked like the dad and one of the boys left during the sermon and the mom and the other boy scooted out pretty quickly. Was anyone able to catch them?"

Shannon spoke up: "Elizabeth Jenkins sat behind them and talked to them in the lobby. God really had Elizabeth in the right spot last week because she noticed one of their boys is a lot like her nephew who has autism. She got their contact info and sent it to me Sunday afternoon. Their last name is Miller. Grant and Jessica are the parents, and their sons are Zach and Levi. Zach is in seventh grade, and Levi is in fourth. I'll be reaching out this week with the next steps they can take to join us for Sunday school if they're ready. Tyler, Zach will be in your middle school class."

"Great!" replied the youth pastor, Tyler. "I'll watch for him and introduce him around. I'm planning to make an announcement about the upcoming buddy training for our high schoolers who are interested. Let's talk later about how I can best phrase a few things so I'm sensitive to the siblings in the room."

"Sounds good," Shannon replied. "Actually, I had lunch last week with our new admin assistant, Grace, and she told me she has a brother with Down syndrome. I asked if we could get her opinion on how to best communicate with our special-needs families and talk about our disability ministry. She said she'd be happy to help anytime!"

Pastor Nathan smiled and nodded. "Grace told me about her brother Daniel in her interview. She said growing up as his big sister really shaped her into the person she is today. I'm glad she's willing to help us be sensitive in our communication. Shannon, let me know if I can help you this week as you reach out to the Millers and get your team ready. Tyler, next week you can let us know who Zach may already know so we can facilitate his family meeting with other families who may be able to step in to help if there's a need in the future, like if Zach needs rides on Wednesday nights."

"One more thing before we're done," said Chris. "Since we noticed they didn't make it all the way through the service on Sunday, let's make sure they see the noise-reducing headphones available in the lobby. And they can come to our worship team practice on Wednesday if it would help Levi see the worship center when the lights are all on and there aren't as many people in there. We always enjoy an audience when we're playing and singing!"

Pastor Nathan nodded again. "Good idea! I know we've had other kids sit through your rehearsals so they are more comfortable during the services, so we'll make sure the Millers know it's an option. Good job, guys! Thanks for thinking of so many ways we can help the whole family feel included!"

On her way out of Pastor Nathan's office, Shannon started a group text with Nikki, Angela, and Matt: "In our staff meeting we talked about a new family who visited on Sunday. I'm going to reach out to the family and get more info. Nikki, he's in fourth grade, so he will be in your class. Matt, you're scheduled to be a buddy on Sunday, so I'll let you know what he likes and what he may struggle with when I get their registration form. Angela, let's be prepared for him to join you guys in the sensory room if he needs a break. I'll email on Thursday with more details for everyone!"

From Neglect to Notice to Needs Being Met

Now in these days when the disciples were increasing in number, a complaint by the Hellenists arose against the Hebrews because their widows were being neglected in the daily distribution. And the twelve summoned the full number of the disciples and said, "It is not right that we should give up preaching the word of God to serve tables. Therefore, brothers, pick out from among you seven men of good repute, full of the Spirit and of wisdom, whom we will appoint to this duty. But we will devote ourselves to prayer and to the ministry of the word." And what they said pleased the whole gathering, and they chose Stephen, a man full of faith and of the Holy Spirit, and Philip, and Prochorus, and Nicanor, and Timon, and Parmenas, and Nicolaus, a proselyte of Antioch. These they set before the apostles, and they prayed and laid their hands on them.

And the word of God continued to increase, and the number of the disciples multiplied greatly in Jerusalem, and a great many of the priests became obedient to the faith. (Acts 6:1–7)

In Acts 6 the church was growing, but one group was feeling neglected: the Hellenistic widows. The apostles weren't being malicious; they were simply so busy with the growth of the church that they didn't notice a group of people was going unnoticed. The issue was brought to their attention, and they responded by appointing specific men to meet the need. The result: "And the word of God continued to increase, and the number of the disciples multiplied greatly in Jerusalem" (Acts 6:7). These men advocated for the Hellenistic widows. In our churches today, special-needs families also need advocates.[1]

Everyone has a part to play in making special-needs families feel included—ministerial staff, support staff, teachers, and volunteers. In this chapter we'll think about the possible positions on your church's team and how to help all of them feel equipped in their role as advocates.

Who Is on the Team?

I want this book to be helpful to churches of any and every size. In order to be helpful, it needs to include guidance for churches that

---

1 This paragraph is adapted from Sandra Peoples, "What Should I Do If My Church Doesn't Have a Special-Needs Ministry?," Key Ministry, February 22, 2018, https://www.keyministry.org/.

have different numbers of staff positions and volunteer leaders. When we talk about who is on the advocacy team, we're going to start with the children's minister taking the lead to include and welcome all families, then how the church will know when it's time to hand off the ministry to a volunteer leader, and then what it would look like to hire a part-time or full-time disability ministry director. My church has gone through this process, from having a volunteer leader to hiring a part-time inclusion coordinator for special-needs families, so I'll share the lessons we learned along the way.

The Inclusive Children's Ministry Leader

If you're a children's ministry leader who's taking initiative in the area of inclusion, first I want to say thank you! You likely weren't trained in special education or inclusion for people with disabilities, but God has put it on your heart to foster a welcoming place for families, and a lot of the work to make that happen falls to you and your volunteers. You may have picked up this book because you have a kid or two with needs that your volunteers are struggling to meet. Lots of churches become accessible and develop disability ministries because "We have this one kid . . ." I'm so glad you want to learn more about the topic of inclusion and learn how to make your ministry more accessible.

Even though you may be the one taking the lead on implementing the idea of accessibility, you don't have to do it all on your own. One of the beautiful lessons we can learn in disability ministry is that none of us can pretend to be able to meet every need on our own. We were designed to need help from others. Our friends with disabilities can't hide those needs, and we shouldn't hide them either. Including all types of people is at the very heart of God. He will use you to reach families and create an inclusive environment, but he doesn't have to use only you. Follow the example we read about in Acts 6—pray for more advocates and make the need clear to your leadership. This chapter will help you know what qualities to look for in the volunteers who will join you in this advocacy work.

As you take steps toward accessibility, I want to encourage you to have clear conversations with your lead pastor and other decision makers at your church about your capacity to lead in this way. I have encouraged children's ministry leaders to track the time they spend on making their ministries inclusive and let their pastors know when that amount of time reaches a point that isn't sustainable for them. That may be 15 to 25 percent of your work week. Have the conversation when that percentage is low so you don't reach burnout level before you have the help you need.

The staff meeting scenario at the beginning of this chapter is an ideal situation, and it didn't happen overnight. Be encouraged that God sees your work. He wants what you want—for everyone to be welcome in his church. Proverbs 31:8 says, "Speak up for those who have no voice" (CSB). You are following this biblical principle. You are their voice in staff meetings, when planning for activities and events (like church camp and vacation Bible school), in discussions with volunteers, on stage, in small-group meetings, and anytime they aren't being considered.

Advocacy with Your Pastor and Church Staff

If the focus on inclusion and accessibility is new to your church, here's what your advocacy might look like with your staff and pastor.

With the staff, you might ask questions such as:

- How will this event work for our kids with disabilities?
- Are we providing childcare up to a certain age *and* for kids with special needs?
- What can we do to make sure the Smith family feels welcome?
- Is the space accessible for everyone?
- Does the policy take this variable into consideration?
- Will we need to enlist an extra volunteer?

To your pastor, you might relay the following information:

- Here's the preferred language people with that disability have asked us to use.
- We can say it this way to be more inclusive and kinder.
- We need these adaptive tools to serve more families.
- Here's how we can be sensitive when communicating about miracles, mental-health issues, how bodies can and should function, healing, and suffering (especially long term).

Having a Designated Disability Ministry Leader (Volunteer, Part-Time, or Full-Time)

As Erik Carter writes,

> Numerous congregations have demonstrated that hiring new staff is not a prerequisite for including children with developmental disabilities in their programs. As more children become involved in your congregation, however, it may be beneficial to identify someone whose role is to ensure that informational and support needs related to inclusion are being addressed.[2]

When you reach the point of needing someone in a role that focuses on supporting people with disabilities and their families, here are some steps you can take.

First, the disability ministry leader is often a person who has a disability, has a family member with a disability, is a special-education teacher, or is a therapy provider (whether occupational, behavioral, speech, or physical). Because disability ministry is a growing field, there are not (yet) many people with degrees in disability ministry. But there are training opportunities, certification options, and even classes available. (You can find out more at accessible-church.com.)

What can be more important than education and even a lot of experience in the field of disability ministry or special education are the characteristics we're looking for in a ministry leader. At our church, we wanted someone who was kind, teachable, cre-

---

2 Erik W. Carter, *Including People with Disabilities in Faith Communities: A Guide for Service Providers, Families, and Congregations* (Paul H. Brooks, 2007), 92.

ative, patient, flexible, and familiar with disability-related terms and the challenges that special-needs families face. Even though our disability ministry doesn't serve only children, the disability ministry leader works most closely with our children's ministry director, so it's helpful that they have a good working relationship.

You know the needs of your church and your ministry, so your expectations should fit your needs. When my church was ready to hire someone part-time to fill this role, we first talked about the job title. We decided on the job title "Inclusion Coordinator for Special Needs Families" because we wanted the ministry leader to think about how to holistically care for the entire family and not just the person with disabilities. Based on the church's size and needs at that time, the expectation was that he or she would be an hourly employee who worked about fifteen hours a week, including Sunday mornings and Wednesday nights.

Here's the sample job description we developed:

- Schedule volunteers for Sunday mornings: specialized children's class, reverse inclusion teenage class, and buddies in the inclusive classes as needed
- Oversee two paid positions on Sunday morning and one on Wednesday nights
- Recruit and train new volunteers (communicate with pastoral staff about needs)
- Monitor the church email address to communicate with parents and church staff
- Develop goals for ministry participants and communicate those goals with children's and youth ministry staff and volunteers

- Organize four respite nights a year
- Organize two community outreaches a year
- Manage the disability ministry budget
- Train and oversee buddies for vacation Bible school
- Be available for consultations with families as needed

As your church welcomes more families and expands what they can offer, this role can expand as well. I have friends who are ministry leaders at large churches who are also hosting resource fairs for families to connect with what's available in their areas. Some are organizing weekly Bible studies for special-needs parents and hosting support groups in their churches. In chapter 7 you'll meet ministry leaders who are managing cafes in their churches that employ adults with disabilities and are offering other weekly opportunities for employment and connection.

I tell our church that God is going to grow our disability ministry at the rate we are willing and available to serve families with care. The more support we have, the more we can expand. And that support includes training everyone on the best practices for inclusion. The ministry leader, whether that's the children's ministry director or a part-time or full-time designated disability ministry leader, relies on the team to make sure programing is accessible. That team includes volunteers already serving in children's and youth ministry who may need to learn inclusive practices and specialized volunteers like teen and adult buddies who are there to focus specifically on those who need extra help. Let's consider how we train the existing team members and then the four steps to adding specialized team members.

Training Everyone on Best Practices for Inclusion

When your church is taking steps to be more inclusive, you will have teachers currently serving in your ministry who will need training to best support students with disabilities. Some of these teachers and volunteers may have been serving for decades. At our church, the teacher for our fifth graders is teaching the kids of parents she taught when they were in fifth grade! I know you are thankful for the years of service some of your teachers have given to your church. And as we train them, we want to be respectful of their experience while expanding the ways they support kids.

As the ministry leader, you can communicate the reasons why your church wants to be more accessible to kids with a variety of extra needs and to their families. It's truly a gospel issue. We want these families to have access to the gospel and a gospel-centered church family. Once you've helped your volunteers understand the reasons for inclusion, then you can prepare them with the methods. It's helpful to host a training at the start of a new school year that covers best practices for accessibility. We also take advantage of vacation Bible school training to share methods and practices with teachers and volunteers. If you can't do this in person, you can record a video to show your team and then follow up to see whether they have any questions. If you don't feel equipped to lead the training yourself, you can contact your denomination or association to see whether they recommend anyone to train your team or suggest you reach out to a parachurch organization like Key Ministry, Joni and Friends, Ability Ministry, Guidelight, The Banquet Network, SOAR Special Needs, or others listed on the resource page at accessible-church.com.

Another resource you can give your existing teachers and volunteers is the addition of buddies to help kids and students who would benefit from extra attention and help. Let's think about the role of a buddy and how to support them.

Adding Specialized Team Members: Buddies

Remember in chapter 1 when we read about Moses and God discussing God's instruction to Moses about approaching Pharaoh and asking him to let his people go? Moses used his limitation as an excuse not to fulfill the calling God gave him. Instead of excusing Moses, God supplied a helper—Moses's brother Aaron. God told Moses, "You shall speak to him and put the words in his mouth, and I will be with your mouth and with his mouth and will teach you both what to do. He shall speak for you to the people, and he shall be your mouth, and you shall be as God to him" (Ex. 4:15–16). Moses had a calling he didn't believe he could fulfill on his own. God provided Aaron, who was strong where Moses was weak. This partnership between Moses and Aaron is the foundation for the buddy partnership between kids and teens who need extra help at church and the teens and adults who partner with them. Let's first talk about what we look for in a buddy and what their role is, then we'll go through four steps for including them (and other volunteers) in your ministry.

The role of a buddy is to make the gospel accessible and understandable, to ensure the safety of the child they are buddying (and the other children), to provide support, to empower giftedness, to encourage socialization, to anticipate triggers, to have compassion during times of stress, and to work with teachers and ministry leaders to find solutions to ongoing challenges.[3] A buddy can either be one on one with a child or be a floater buddy who is in a classroom ready to offer help to anyone who needs it. During vacation Bible school, we have floater buddies in as many classes as possible as we get to know the kids and figure out who will need extra help.

What do buddies need to be successful? They need to know their role and how they fit into the structure of the class and overall ministry. They need to feel comfortable asking questions and know who the best person is to answer their questions: Is it the classroom teacher? The ministry director? They need a plan for many possible scenarios. They need to feel empowered to make quick decisions. And they need tools, like a buddy bag.[4]

The buddies in our ministry carry buddy bags, which are cinch backpacks with sensory tools such as fidget toys, noise-reducing headphones, visual schedules, and a visual timer. The buddy offers these tools to the student when needed. The bag also includes a lanyard with information about the child, including likes, dislikes, triggers, and his or her spiritual goals (more about this in chapter 5). When our buddies check in on Sunday mornings in the sensory room, they grab a bag, make sure it has everything needed, and join the person they are buddying with or the classroom they will be supporting.

---

3   Adapted from a training led by Stephen "Doc" Hunsley of SOAR Special Needs and Beth Golik of Key Ministry at Inclusion Fusion Life, 2019, available at https://static1 .squarespace.com/static/56d87a50d210b825aa8f70a9/t/5cb1fb97419202e78f397a2a /1555168187987/Starting+a+Special+Needs+Ministry+for+IFL2019.pdf.

4   Sandra Peoples, "Recruiting, Training, and Supporting Buddies in Your Church," Key Ministry, August 24, 2021, https://www.keyministry.org/.

In addition to the general children's ministry or youth ministry training that the buddies participate in, we have a few policies we've created specifically for them (especially for our teens who serve as buddies). They can't be on their phones when they are volunteering, and they can't take pictures of or with the person they are buddying. We also talk to them about having conversations with others about the kids they support that might potentially be embarrassing or personal. We are especially sensitive to this if they are in a life group with the child's parents or if they are in youth group with the child's siblings.

Now that you understand the role of being a buddy and their responsibilities, let's talk about four steps to volunteer assimilation for these buddies and all of our ministry helpers.

Four Steps to Volunteer Assimilation

Volunteers are a very important part of any ministry, and it takes four steps of caring for them to make sure that they feel supported and successful. The first step is *recruiting*, the second step is *training*, the third step is *supporting*, and the final step is *celebrating*. Let's look at each of these four steps for success for our volunteers.

The first step to success is recruiting. There are at least five ways to recruit volunteers. The first is word of mouth from your current volunteers. The best way to get new volunteers is for the current volunteers who serve in your ministry to tell their friends how much fun it is to be part of your ministry. They can tell their small groups or Sunday school classes, "It is so much fun serving in the disability ministry. You should come serve with us!" Word of mouth is a great way to recruit new volunteers.

The second way to recruit volunteers is to invite them to sign up for a low-commitment opportunity. It can be hard to enlist a volunteer if they think they have to serve every week or every other week. But if you can get them to say yes to a low-commitment opportunity, to show them what it looks like to serve one time, then they may be more likely to commit to being a regular volunteer. Low-commitment opportunities include respite events, vacation Bible school, or another event that you're doing through your disability ministry. Get them to say yes to helping one night at a respite event, and then maybe you can plug them in more consistently on Sunday mornings.

The next way is ministry visibility when other areas are also recruiting new volunteers. My church hosts a Serve Sunday every year, when the ministry leaders set up tables to share what their needs are and answer questions about what it's like to serve in their ministry area. If your church has an opportunity like that, make sure you're part of it! You could also talk to the staff about making an announcement about your needs to the congregation on a Sunday morning or recording a video that can be played in the services and on social media.

The fourth idea has a high success rate but can feel like the hardest (especially for introverts). It is to *identify* and *ask*. At our church we have the most success with identifying somebody we think would be great in the ministry and then asking that person to consider serving. Some people don't even realize that they have the skills that would be a great fit for our ministry. Such an invitation can give them the confidence to say yes.

The last idea is filling in around paid positions. If you're having trouble getting enough help, consider hiring people who will be there every week and then support them with volunteers. Having a few consistent people in place can help get more volunteers because they know there's a lead teacher in the room who knows the kids well and is prepared to present the lesson.

The second step to successful volunteer assimilation is training. We have policies in place for all our volunteers to follow, and we make sure as part of the training process that they understand all those policies. They also get background checks and do MinistrySafe training. We have big training events twice a year and use videos on specific topics to supplement that training (either videos we've recorded or video resources we've found and shared). The video option is especially helpful if you're onboarding volunteers at different times throughout the year.

Another way we train is by shadowing. On a Sunday morning, we pair together an experienced buddy with someone who is training so the new volunteer sees what the role looks like. As I mentioned in the section above on recruiting, we also use respite nights and vacation Bible school as opportunities for training. The transition to helping consistently on Sunday mornings is much easier when they've had experience through these other opportunities.

The third step to success for our volunteers is supporting them. Our job isn't done once we recruit and train them. They need ongoing support so they feel successful week after week and so they don't burn out in the ministry. Part of this support is providing them consistent, clear communication. We have a saying in our family and at our church: Clear communication is kind.

We don't want our volunteers guessing at anything! We want them to know exactly where they're going on a Sunday morning, exactly who they're going to talk to, what their check-in process is, what room they go to get the buddy bag, and what fidgets to put in the buddy bag (if they need to fill it up themselves). The more communication we can give ahead of time, the more comfortable they feel and the more likely they are to be successful in our ministries.

We also want to ensure they're comfortable asking questions (even sensitive questions), making a suggestion for a change, or offering constructive criticism. When I oversaw the ministry at our current church, we made sure our volunteers knew they could come to me or the children's ministry director with any questions or issues they had. Because I'm also the pastor's wife, I didn't want anyone to feel weird about something they wanted to communicate. Even though we have a part-time paid staff person in that position now, we still let volunteers know that anyone on the team is happy to answer questions, help brainstorm solutions, or hear suggestions for changes or improvements.

The last step in assimilating our volunteers is celebration. We can't forget to celebrate how important their service is to our ministry and to celebrate what is happening in the lives of our friends with disabilities and their entire families. Here are a few ways we can celebrate our volunteers.

First, we can give lots of specific verbal praise. We can tell them they're doing a great job by noticing something specific they did and letting them know how much we appreciate it. That praise could sound like this: "Hey, I saw you with Michael earlier! It looked like he was reluctant to get to the classroom, but you came up with a great idea to help get him in there by 'dropping' blocks down the hall. He picked up the blocks on the way to his room, and then he got to build a tower. That was so creative of you! Thank you so much for how you handled that situation." The more we can be on the lookout for specific things to praise them for, the more encouraged they will feel. You could consider having a volunteer of the week that you praise publicly (in an email newsletter or in a Facebook group for your church). If you can give a specific reason why that person is the volunteer of the week, like the example with Michael picking up blocks on his way to the classroom, your appreciation can also inspire creativity in other volunteers.

You could also show thanks with tangible gifts or by hosting events to build relationships. Give each volunteer a candy bar or a coffee gift card one week. Or offer a thank-you breakfast before church. You could also invite the kids and their families to write thank-you notes for the volunteers. It doesn't have to cost a lot of money, but even small ways to say thank you can mean a lot.

And finally, remind them they are part of a bigger story, a movement of inclusion and accessibility that provides gospel hope. Volunteers want to feel like they're doing something important in your church and in the life of the families they are supporting. Point out to your team, "The Roberts family wouldn't be able to attend week after week if we didn't have the sensory class available. Thanks for your consistent help!" We all want to be part of what God is doing and how he is using the gifts of his people. Remind your volunteers of that bigger purpose so they are encouraged.

These four steps of assimilation success for volunteers—recruiting, training, supporting, and celebrating—apply to our disability ministry volunteers or any volunteers we have in children's ministry, preschool ministry, or youth ministry. We can build a strong team in which members understand their roles as advocates and take steps toward accessibility for all our ministry participants.

Bringing It All Together

Based on what you learned in this chapter, here are steps of accessibility you can take:

Start by evaluating who will be part of your ministry team as you take steps of increased accessibility.

Then try recruiting and training buddies to help kids and teens in inclusive classes and activities.

Next, apply what you've learned by training all your volunteers on best practices for inclusion.

5

Student Support

The Goal Is the Gospel

AFTER THE STAFF MEETING, Shannon got back to her office and texted Jessica to introduce herself as the children's ministry director. After a few texts back and forth, Jessica said they would be interested in Levi participating in the children's ministry options that Sunday. Shannon emailed her a link to the online children's ministry registration form that included questions about Levi's needs. Jessica filled it out that evening. Shannon texted again the next morning to let Jessica know they would have a buddy ready to hang out with Levi during small-group time. She sent Jessica a link to a social story she could print out and show to Levi so he would be prepared. She also invited them to come by the church on Thursday after school so Levi could see the classroom he would be in and the sensory room where he could take a break if he needed it.

The next Sunday, Elizabeth and her son Gerald were greeters in the children's area, so there was a friendly face at the door when Jessica, Grant, Zach, and Levi walked in. Gerald and Zach recognized each other from their science class, so Gerald asked his mom if he could walk Zach over to the middle school room. Levi was excited to meet his buddy, Matt, and head to his class with him. Jessica and Grant tried to hang out in the lobby "just in case," but Elizabeth invited them to her life group. Shannon promised to text them if necessary. Jessica and Grant sat down in the life group and looked at each other as they exhaled and let their tense shoulders drop. They both knew it was a huge step for their family to all feel comfortable and welcome at church. This could be the beginning of a new season for all of them.

Levi and his buddy, Matt, walked down the hall to the third-and-fourth-grade classroom. Matt had read the info that Jessica shared on Levi's registration form, so he had prepared a buddy bag with noise-reducing headphones, fidgets, a visual timer, and some sour candy (Levi's favorite). One of Levi's special interests was maps, so as they walked into their classroom, Matt showed Levi the map of the building they were in, which showed the fire exits. Nikki, the classroom teacher, approached to meet Levi. After welcoming him to the class, she pointed out the visual schedule she had on the wall. "Right now everyone is drawing pictures of their favorite foods. In a few minutes we're going to talk about our favorite foods and some that we don't like. You and Matt can work together to draw your favorite foods or talk about them together."

Nikki got the class's attention and asked each person to stand up and name one of their favorite foods. Then she asked the rest of the class to stand up if they also liked that food or to sit down if they didn't like it. When Levi's turn came, he said his favorite food was mac and cheese. "Stand up if you also like mac and cheese," said Ms. Nikki. Levi was sure everyone would like mac and cheese as much as he did, but one girl sat down. She said it was gross. Matt could tell this frustrated Levi. Levi kept talking to Matt about mac and cheese even after Ms. Nikki had moved on. He scribbled on the paper where he and Matt had drawn a bowl of mac and cheese. Matt whispered to Levi, "I can tell you're getting frustrated. If you can stop scribbling on the paper, we can walk to the sensory room for a break. I'll tell Ms. Nikki we'll be back in ten minutes."

On their way out of the classroom, Matt and Levi saw Shannon and told her they were on their way to the sensory room. Shannon was prepared with a way to pique Levi's interests to go back into his class when his break was over: "It's a great idea to go jump on the trampoline when you get frustrated! But when it's time to go back, Ms. Nikki will be talking about Daniel and his friends. They had to move away from their homes to a new place. I printed off a map that shows where they lived in Judah and where they moved to in Babylon. You can look at it with Matt and then show it to Ms. Nikki when you get back to your class. She will be excited for you to show it to her!"

Matt and Levi got to the sensory room, where Ms. Angela and her class were also talking about Daniel and his friends. Matt set the visual timer for ten minutes, and Levi went straight for the trampoline. He noticed that Ms. Angela had different vegetables that her class was smelling, touching, and tasting. She told them, "Daniel and his friends ate only vegetables and drank only water when they got to Babylon because some of the food and drink they were given was considered unclean by God's rules at the time. By following God's instructions about what they ate while they were in Babylon, they learned God's way is best." Levi went to the table, and Ms. Grace, Ms. Angela's helper that week, put some veggies in a bowl for him to try.

After ten minutes, the timer beeped, and Levi was ready to go back to class. He remembered the map Ms. Shannon had given him and was excited to look at it more and show it to Ms. Nikki. Levi and Matt passed Ms. Shannon again in the hall, and Levi told her that he tasted cucumbers but didn't like the smell of broccoli. She asked if he knew why Daniel and his friends only ate vegetables. He replied, "Because God's way is best!" She gave him a high five and said Ms. Nikki's class was watching a video about Daniel and his friends that Levi would like.

Matt and Levi were quiet as they walked back into the dark room and sat at the table. Levi did like the video, and when it was over, Ms. Nikki talked about how Daniel and his friends moved a long way from their home. She asked if Levi wanted to come up and show his map to the class. Ms. Nikki's helper, Mr. Scott, handed out maps like Levi's to everyone so they could see them too. Levi talked about how far Judah was from Babylon and how long it might have taken them to walk all that way.

When Levi sat back down, Ms. Nikki talked about Daniel and his friends eating just vegetables and drinking just water so they kept following God's protective rules about healthy food and drinks at that time. She also told the class, "God's way is best!" They talked through some situations the kids faced where they had to decide whether they should do what God would want them to do or do what other people told them to do. Then they got into two groups and raced to find and read two verses that went along with their lesson about Daniel: Romans 12:1 and

Proverbs 3:5–6. Levi's team didn't win, which was frustrating to him, but Matt said that maybe next week they would play a different game and win. Matt also said it was time for all the classes to come together for music in the big room. He gave Levi noise-reducing headphones and let him pick a fidget toy. They talked about how Levi could let Matt know if the noise hurt his ears, and they could take another break in the sensory room if they needed to.

When Jessica and Grant peeked into the room where Levi was, he and Matt were standing in the back of the room where there were fewer kids, but he looked like he was enjoying listening to the music. They had talked to Shannon on their way to see Levi, and she told him how he had done that morning. They all agreed it was a great first Sunday experience for Levi. When it was time to go, Jessica and Grant asked Levi if he wanted to stop by the sensory room again on their way to the service and jump on the trampoline for five minutes. He agreed, and during the service that day, he had an easier time sitting still. He enjoyed music time more because he had grabbed a pair of noise-reducing headphones on their way into the worship center, but when it was time to sit still and listen to the sermon, he felt anxious. Shannon had told Jessica and Grant that Levi would be welcome back in the sensory class during the sermon time if that worked best for him. So Grant walked him over to see Ms. Angela again, and then Grant was able to sit with Jessica and Zach for the sermon for the first time in years.

On the way home, both boys couldn't stop talking about the people they met, the fun they had, and what they learned. Levi was excited to tell them all that "God's way is best!"

Adapting for Every Learner

> If I speak in the tongues of men and of angels, but have not love, I am a noisy gong or a clanging cymbal. . . .
>
> Now, brothers, if I come to you speaking in tongues, how will I benefit you unless I bring you some revelation or knowledge or prophecy or teaching? . . . So with yourselves, if with your tongue you utter speech that is not intelligible, how will anyone know what is said? For you will be speaking into the air. There are doubtless many different languages in the world, and none is without meaning, but if I do not know the meaning of the language, I will be a foreigner to the speaker and the speaker a foreigner to me. So with yourselves, since you are eager for manifestations of the Spirit, strive to excel in building up the church. (1 Cor. 13:1; 14:6, 9–12)

In our children's ministry environments, we don't want it to be said that we are "speaking into the air" because the kids that God has brought to us that week aren't able to understand what we're saying or get the point of the lesson and the activities we planned around the lesson. We want each one of them to be drawn by the Spirit into more knowledge and a deeper understanding of God's love for them. But how do we meet the needs of the diverse group of learners we have? And how do we know what they can learn, what challenges they face, and what our expectations should be? We're going to answer these questions and more in this chapter. My prayer is that by the end of it, you'll feel equipped to meet the needs of each child whom God brings into your ministry.

The first step in adapting our teaching is to remember children with disabilities reflect the image of God and have the potential to have a relationship with him and grow in Christlikeness. When we can see the image of God in all children, then we can work to "re-story" the challenges they face to focus on their good design by a loving Creator. As we read about in chapter 1, when Jesus and his disciples encountered a man who was born blind, the disciples' focus on deficits and blame was shifted to God's design and purpose for the man (John 9). Teachers can do that for their students as well. But when teachers and volunteers see the *imago Dei* in each child and remember he or she was designed on purpose for a purpose, they are motivated to support that child to the best of their ability.

Factors That Influence a Child's Ability to Learn

Jared Kennedy writes in *Keeping Your Children's Ministry on Mission*, "We need to present engaging, Christ-centered lessons to children, but they need to be *developmentally appropriate*."[1] Cognitive, moral, spiritual, social, emotional, and physical development happens at different speeds for children. Girls often mature faster than boys. Physical development can be influenced by nutrition and activity levels. And cognitive development includes skills that are influenced by many factors, including trust for the teacher, support at home, and genetic predispositions.

Keeping up with all the diversity in the Sunday school classroom—including physical and cognitive disabilities, mental health diagnoses, behavioral diagnoses, and learning disabilities, plus

---

1   Jared Kennedy, *Keeping Your Children's Ministry on Mission: Practical Strategies for Discipling the Next Generation* (Crossway, 2022), 121.

developmental stages, learning styles, and motivational behaviors—can feel overwhelming. Especially for volunteer leaders. But these children will be present in our churches, and it's better to be proactive about meeting their needs than to be reactive. As we read about in the parable of the great banquet in Luke 14, after first inviting people with disabilities the servant said, "Still there is room."

When ministry leaders likewise show acceptance and hospitality to people with disabilities, and thus make accommodations for them, there is still room for everyone. Those accommodations do not take away from what is needed by most people. In many cases, it can enhance their experience as well. The key to not feeling overwhelmed is to simply get to know each student and do your best to meet his or her needs.

Academic Challenges and Solutions (Applying UDL Principles)

If I want to get from Houston to Dallas—let's say I want to visit my son who is in college there—I have different travel options. I could drive, following one of multiple routes that all take about four and a half hours. I could fly, which would take a little over an hour. I could take a bus, which would take four to five hours but leaves at only certain times. I could ride a bike; Apple Maps says that would take me twenty-five hours, which doesn't include all the breaks I would need. Or I could even walk; Apple Maps says that would take a hundred and four hours, which again doesn't include breaks.

With all those options for traveling from Houston to Dallas, what factors would influence my choice? They could include: the length of time the trip would take, my budget, whether I was doing strength training, my need to have a car available when I got there, the sights I would want to see, who would be traveling with me, obstacles in my way (like construction), the time of day I needed to arrive, the weather or time of year I was traveling, and what I was taking with me (like just a backpack versus hauling a trailer). Even with all the routes and options, the destination is the same—seeing my son.

At its core, the teaching approach known as "universal design for learning" (UDL) employs a similar concept. It provides multiple ways to achieve the learning goal. Tracy McElhatten, who works with Lifeway to adapt curriculum for kids with special needs, says UDL comes from the concept of universal design, which is about architecture. Think of how everyone can use a ramp to access a stage but only some people can use stairs. UDL applies that concept to education—making sure that everyone can access the classroom and the curriculum in a meaningful way. And this design purposefully meets the needs of all learners and is not an afterthought.[2] It includes multiple means of *engagement* (the *why* of learning), multiple means of *representation* (the *what* of learning), and multiple means of *action and expression* (the *how* of learning).[3]

Jesus himself used teaching methods that look like UDL in action. He taught in different ways and in various locations. There were sermons to crowds and private conversations. They happened at tables, temples, and on mountainsides. He piqued interest with

---

2   Sandra Peoples in Tracy McElhattan, "Engaging and Inclusive Teaching Models," *Key Ministry: The Podcast*, episode 95, https://www.keyministry.org/.

3   "The UDL Guidelines," UDL Guidelines, https://udlguidelines.cast.org.

parables (the prodigal son), miracles (walking on water), and modeling the behavior he wanted his followers to emulate (washing the disciples' feet). He used multiple representations, including poetry (the Sermon on the Mount), quotations and allusions to familiar stories in the Hebrew Bible ("Remember Lot's wife"; Luke 17:32) and memorable similes ("The kingdom of heaven is like treasure hidden in a field"; Matt. 13:44). And he told his followers that they would have opportunities to show what they had learned from him: "Truly, truly, I say to you, whoever believes in me will also do the works that I do; and greater works than these will he do, because I am going to the Father" (John 14:12).

Jesus's message was so important that he wanted everyone to understand and apply what they learned. Jesus intentionally adapted his teaching, the environment, and how he asked people to respond because he knew that every person had different needs and he wanted to meet people where they were. He always adapted, sought people, and met needs. We can learn from his example to teach in a wide variety of ways and give our kids opportunities to apply what they have learned.

Applying UDL principles can follow these simple steps:

1. Focus on one goal for the lesson
2. Think of the multiple ways kids could get to that goal
3. Provide them with those multiple paths
4. Check for understanding
5. Give multiple opportunities for application and action

Many curriculum options follow UDL principles even if they don't explicitly say so. In the Bible Studies for Life curriculum from Lifeway that my church uses, I always flip to the section in the back titled "Suggestions for Including Children with Special Needs" to help me focus on one main idea and get an idea for another example or activity that would support that main idea. In your inclusive classrooms, you can get to know each student individually and provide pathways of understanding and application for the lessons.

Individual Spiritual Plans

You may be thinking that it's too much to keep up with all the needs the kids have and all the ways we could meet those needs. How can a volunteer teacher who sees the kids for just a few hours a week remember everything he or she would need to in order to teach every student? There's a solution that works for churches of every size! Because every child is unique, we have developed ISPs for each one—individual spiritual plans. Similar to what the students have at school under their IEPs (individualized education programs), our ISPs take into consideration their likes, dislikes, strengths, goals, and behaviors. We decide on the goals after we get to know the student and by talking to the parents about what goals they have while their child is with us at church.[4]

When setting the goals for the student, we remember the primary goal—sharing the gospel! Everything is for the purpose of the student being able to hear and respond to the gospel. The goals at school, therapy, and home will meet a variety of needs

4   Content in this paragraph is adapted from Sandra Peoples, "Creating ISPs (Individualized Spiritual Plans!) for Every Student in Your Special-Needs Ministry," Key Ministry, June 18, 2020, https://www.keyministry.org/.

for the students, so it's important that we stay focused on our ISP goals because students are with us for such a short time compared to how much time they spend other places.

To create a rubric of ideas for ISP goals, you can think of all the different activities and opportunities you have for your kids at church.[5] Then you can list possible goals in order of the support needed. Let's say one of your priorities is Scripture memorization. What would it look like for different types of learners with different ability levels to be able to memorize Scripture? Here's what the personalized goals could be if a student isn't able to memorize a verse independently:

- Listen to friends repeating the verse while following along as a teacher or buddy points to the words (on the board, in a workbook, or on a handout).
- Use a communication device or sign language to communicate the Bible memory verse.
- Fill in the blanks of the verse using words or pictures/ PECS (picture exchange communication system).
- Repeat the Bible memory verse with prompting after each word or each group of words.
- Memorize a shortened version of the verse or passage.
- Sing along to a song that includes the verse.

The process for setting ISP goals takes a few steps over time. First, we take into consideration the information on the registration form that the child's parents have filled out. Then we

---

5   You can see a sample ISP rubric at accessible-church.com.

observe the child in the type of class we think best fits his or her needs (in the inclusive class with a buddy, in the specialized sensory class, or in both environments). Next we sit down with the parents (and the child if he or she wants to be involved) and talk about the opportunities we have for the discipleship of their child. We want to partner with them in this responsibility, so we share what we've observed and what we think the goals could be in each category. When we're in agreement, we create a bio sheet for our kids in the sensory room that we have available in a folder or a small version that fits into a pouch on a lanyard for our kids who get support from a buddy. That lanyard is placed in a buddy bag that includes the tools that would help support that student.

Bio Sheets and Buddy Bag Lanyards

To help teachers in the sensory classroom and help buddies in the inclusive classroom get to know the kids they are supporting, we create bio sheets and lanyards. They include:

- name
- parents' names
- parents' contact info
- allergies/medical issues
- likes
- dislikes

- spiritual goals
- additional info
- student's schedule

Here's what the bio sheet looked like for my son James when he was younger:[6]

1. James Peoples (with his picture so new volunteers can get to know him quickly)
2. Parents: Pastor Lee and Sandra
3. Contact info: (my phone number here)
4. Allergies/medical issues: none
5. Likes: tickles, puzzles, swinging, trains, music, snack time
6. Dislikes: waiting, loud noises, coloring/writing
7. Spiritual goals: for James to hear that Jesus loves him, repeat a Bible memory verse each week, pray with prompting, identify by name friends and helpers at church, and learn the words and motions to the songs we sing
8. Additional info: goes to the bathroom independently
9. James's schedule: in the sensory classrooms both hours

6   See Peoples, "Creating ISPs."

These goals can be adjusted at any time. The classroom teacher, buddy, student, or parents can let us know that they'd like to talk about a change, and we go through the steps to update them. We also reflect on the goals and talk about changes when it's time for a transition between classes (from second grade to third grade) or ministries (from children's ministry to youth ministry). This doesn't have to be a formal process. We often all agree that a student needs more independence or raised expectations, and then we try it out for a few weeks to see how it goes.

Learning and discipleship are important parts of supporting students, but we also want to be prepared to support positive behavior choices and reduce distracting behavior. The ways we support their behavior can also go on their bio sheets or lanyard cards. Let's talk about the importance of being behavior investigators and how we can see behavior as communication.

Behavior Challenges and Solutions

Our kids (as well as teens and adults) have three needs to be comfortable in our ministry environments: safety, social connection, and success. These cover sensory needs, community needs, and academic needs. Our classrooms and activity spaces can offer protection, affirmation, and motivation to help kids meet their needs. When those needs aren't met—whether that reason is environmental or due to the limitations of the child's disability—the child communicates the lack of safety, social connection, and success through his or her behavior. Children's ministry leader Kim Botto shares, "Children are communicating their fears, their anxieties, and their feelings, but they are not using their words.

They are using their behavior. We need to listen to what they are saying through their behavior—the only language that may be accessible to them in the moment."[7]

Behavior specialists will tell us that our behavior communicates a need for something that can be measured (like a tangible object) to meet a physical or sensory need; to escape a demand, an activity, or a sensory stimulation; or to get attention from adults or peers. To figure out what the behavior is communicating, we need to become behavior investigators. What's the best tool for behavior investigation? Remembering the ABCs of behavior:

Antecedent: What happened before?
Behavior: What was the behavior?
Consequences: What happened after?

When a child exhibits a behavior we want to decrease, we look for what happened before that behavior and what happened after. You can change the antecedent (what came before) or the consequence (what came after). The student changes the behavior. In our investigation, we want to identify the need (if possible), notice triggers, and pay attention to the consequences (how the child may be getting the need met in a way that perpetuates the behavior). Let's look at some examples.

Consider this situation: A five-year-old kindergartner won't go in the classroom on a Sunday morning. First, what's the motivation? It could be she enjoys the attention she's getting from Mom

7   Kim Botto, "Treasure or Troublemaker?," keynote session at Key Ministry's Disability and the Church Conference, April 28–29, 2023, published on May 7, 2023; available at https://vimeo.com/824507513.

and Dad. Her brothers and sisters have gone to their classes, and all of Mom and Dad's attention is on her. They are speaking in their kindest voices because it's Sunday, and they are parenting in front of a crowd of people in the lobby. Or she may not feel safe when she's separated from her parents. She's gotten used to it on school days, but it's harder at church, where she goes only once a week.

Here are some steps we could take to help her feel safe and, hopefully, adjust her behavior. Quickly transition Mom and Dad away by letting them know we can handle helping their daughter. Make the hall fun on the way to her classroom. Can we skip down the hall? Can we play I Spy? Can we create a map and let her follow it? We could give her a task so when she gets to her classroom, she gets attention and praise from her teacher. I might hand her a dry-erase marker and tell her that Mr. John really needs that marker to teach their class that day. (I've let Mr. John know ahead of time that if a child gives him anything, he needs to be super excited to receive whatever it is.) You could also ask Mom and Dad to take a selfie when they get to their class and text it to you so you can show her that Mom and Dad are having a good time in their class.

Or maybe you have a fifth-grade boy in a class with kids at multiple ages. He's a smart kid, and he's getting bored. His need for success isn't being met because the class doesn't feel challenging to him. So he answers every question from the teacher by calling out in a bored voice. What is his motivation? It could be attention, distraction, or to speed up lesson time to get back to something more fun. To help decrease this behavior, you could adjust how you ask questions. Put a task with your ask, like,

"Everyone give a thumbs up if you think that Jonah should have gone to Ninevah or a thumbs down if you think it was a good idea for him to try to hide from God on a boat," or, "Stand up if you think God made fish on the fifth day." With these options, you are giving fewer opportunities for the behavior you want to decrease. You can also set a clear expectation of behavior and then reward what you want to see. If he calls out, ignore his reply and give someone raising a hand the opportunity to answer. Or you could offer alternatives to shouting out, telling him to whisper to his buddy or write down a list of his answers.

Being a behavior investigator means we observe all we can, make a plan, and be prepared to try a few ideas until we find the solution! When it feels challenging or the behavior increases, you can ask for help. Ask the parents whether their child exhibits the same behavior at home or at school and see what solutions work for them. Talk to the teachers and volunteers who know the student well and ask what ideas they have. You can even find a behavioral therapist in your area to come in and observe. We have done that at my church a few times when we've been stumped, and it has always been really helpful.

Final Thoughts on Student Support

You may face some challenges to the process of getting a child or teen in the ministry environment that's the best fit with appropriate ISP goals and the behavior support he or she needs. Now we'll consider some of the challenges I've faced and the solutions that worked.

The first challenge is that there's no known diagnosis. You may see signs of a delay or disability that the child's parents don't yet see. Or you may suspect there's a diagnosis that the parents aren't sharing with you. But do you need a diagnosis in order to offer support? You don't! A diagnosis is a helpful place to start, but it certainly doesn't tell you everything about a child. So even if the child doesn't have a diagnosis, if the parents are in the process of getting a diagnosis, or if you think the parents aren't ready to share a diagnosis yet, you can still put supports in place to help the child.

Second, the child has been in your ministry for years and now needs extra help. It's easier to have a new family who is open about their child's diagnosis start coming to your church because they will take the steps of filling out the registration form and put that diagnosis on the form. But you will likely have families get a diagnosis for their child after he or she has been part of your ministry for a while. Ideally, the parents would feel comfortable talking to you about the diagnosis and communicate with you the challenges they are facing and the solutions they are trying. If that doesn't happen, your next steps will be similar to how you would support a child without a formal diagnosis—you put supports in place to help the child feel safe and connected.

Third, the parents are passive and unhelpful or opinionated and demanding. Either alternative is tough. You may have parents who drop their kid off on a Sunday morning and don't really care what you do to help him. They aren't interested in his ISP, his behavior support plan, or what class he's in. You can still do your best to disciple the child and support his needs without their input. This is also an opportunity for care and discipleship for the parents. The best way to help may be to talk to the leaders of the small group the parents attend and ask whether there is a couple they have connected with in the class who could mentor them. If they seem bitter about their role as special-needs parents, you can facilitate a meeting between them and a more experienced couple who are also special-needs parents.

On the other side of the spectrum, if a child's parents are demanding and argumentative about their daughter's placement or other details you share with them, you can try to listen to the fear behind the anger and help find resolution. At my church, we had a grandmother who would bring her grandson who had intellectual disabilities. He was mostly in the inclusive class with a buddy, but there would be a time each Sunday that he went to the sensory room. She thought going to the sensory room was a punishment for his behavior. We explained his schedule and our goals for him during his time with us. We made sure he didn't miss the lesson time and was able to show her the activity sheet he did with his class each week. This helped her feel better about his inclusion.

The final challenge to address is your church not being able to offer what the child currently needs. This is a hard one, and not everyone in the field of disability ministry agrees on a solution for this challenge. If you're facing this with a family, first pray for them, yourself, and your ministry team. Ask for wisdom on the best way to approach them and who should be with you when you do. I know communicating your limitations as a church is hard, and you want to do it with care and sensitivity. If you can offer alternatives, like paying for a caretaker on Sunday mornings so the rest of the family can attend church together or reminding the mom that she has opportunities for discipleship and friendship at a weekday women's Bible study while her son is at school, that is helpful. There may also be another church in the area that you can connect them with.

If you need to have a tough conversation about why you can't meet their present needs, please do so with sensitivity and with a reminder that even if church isn't accessible to them for a season, Jesus is never far from them. We worship the God who sees and the God who hears. Their family is loved by him. And continue to pray that circumstances will change, and your church will be a good fit at some point.

Bringing It All Together

Based on what you learned in this chapter, here are steps of accessibility you can take:

Start by adjusting your intake form to ask questions about special needs and disabilities.

Then try creating individual spiritual plans for the kids and students currently in your ministry.

Next, apply what you've learned about universal design for learning principles to help the teachers better support all learners.

6

Whole-Family Inclusion

Strengthening Marriages and Supporting Siblings

DURING THE SUMMER MONTHS, my social-media feeds are full of pictures of special-needs families at camps and retreats designed especially for them—from retreats hosted by Guidelight in Oregon to the Baptist Convention of Maryland and Delaware's Everyone Belongs camp, and lots of states in between. Our family attended a Joni and Friends camp in Louisiana a couple years ago, and our son asked to go back every day for months after we got home.

What's so special about these camps and retreats? It starts when the family drives into the campground. They are asked at the entrance, "Do you want a loud or a quiet welcome?" and the answer goes from walkie-talkie to walkie-talkie to the waiting volunteers. When the families turn the corner in their cars, all the volunteers greet them with claps and shouts or with waving hands and smiling faces. Then the helpers who are matched with each family follow behind the family's car in a golfcart and help them unload and get settled. From those first minutes through the whole time together, families like mine are welcomed, served, and celebrated. We know everyone there accepts our family members just as they are and sees their value.

The week we attended camp in Louisiana, I was the speaker for the parent devotion times each day. We gathered to talk about our lives with people who got it. We didn't have to hide the hard parts or keep our worries to ourselves. The stress level of parents of kids with autism is comparable to that of soldiers in active combat.[1] But during our time at camp, we can lower our tense shoulders, turn down the constant vigilance, and experience kindness from the volunteers and empathy from the other parents.

Unfortunately, not every week of the year can be like our time at family retreats. Even on the drive home we're reminded of that as we stop at a fast-food place and get looks when James walks in with his noise-reducing headphones and gets the giggles as we wait for our food. But it can certainly feel more like this in our churches, not just for the person being served by our disability ministries but for everyone in the family.

How people treat our loved one with a disability makes a difference for the whole family. That's why true disability ministry doesn't serve just one person—it serves everyone. Making space at church for the family member with a disability allows each family member to attend. If the church we attended when

---

1   Marsha Mailick Seltzer et al., "Maternal cortisol levels and behavior problems in adolescents and adults with ASD," *Journal of Autism and Developmental Disorders* 40 (2010): 457–69, https://doi.org/10.1007/s10803-009-0887-0.

I was growing up hadn't welcomed my sister, I wouldn't have been able to attend either. It would have changed my family for generations. But thankfully, my whole family could attend, and churches now can have this whole-family approach to disability ministry as well.

The Five Phases of Special-Needs Parenting

In this chapter on family care, we'll look at what I call the five phases of special-needs parenting. Parents go through each phase as they raise their children with disabilities. These phases are helpful to understand so that ministry leaders know better how to support families in these different seasons. I'll share characteristics of the phases, the needs parents have in each one, and how the church can support them along the way. You'll also be able to find resources to support families in each stage at accesiblechurch.com.

As parents of two kids with disabilities, Andrew and Rachel Wilson write, "As we come to terms with our pain and see the love of God at work in spite of it and even through it, we eventually reach the point when we can add our voice to that crowd of witnesses and testify to the ways in which *we* have found God to be faithful."[2] Let's be ready to help the parents we meet at church be part of the witnesses who find God faithful, even in their unexpected circumstances. God is at work in the lives of special-needs families, but they often need support from a church family to recognize that work and progress through these phases.

---

2 Andrew and Rachel Wilson, *The Life We Never Expected: Hopeful Reflections on the Challenges of Parenting Children with Special Needs* (Crossway, 2016), 29.

Phase 1: Recognize Plan B

My parents first heard "Down syndrome" the day my big sister was born in 1977. They didn't know ahead of time that anything would be different about their first child. She was also born with intestinal blockage, a condition that threatened her life. As first-time parents, they found themselves in a plan-B situation they weren't expecting when the labor pains had started the evening before.

We got my son James's autism diagnosis after his third birthday. It wasn't a total surprise because we had seen signs of regression since he had turned two. But there was still an adjustment when it was made official by a school psychologist, occupational therapist, and speech therapist who had interacted with James for only an hour. On diagnosis day, we walked into that school building with concerns and walked out with a label but no idea what his life would look like in the future.

But even though my sister's Down syndrome was a surprise to my parents and James's autism was plan B for us, we soon came to realize it was still God's plan A. These diagnoses weren't mistakes or accidents. They were part of God's plan for our family. My parents had to put that belief into action right away, as a doctor took my dad into a janitorial supply closet and said, "Your daughter has two issues. One is life-threatening, and the other will change your lives forever. If you don't want us to perform the surgery that will save her life, we understand that decision." But my dad said no to the young doctor's offer, and Syble's life was saved through her surgery to fix the intentional blockage. The doctor's warning was also true: Their lives were changed forever. My parents held on to their confidence that God had a plan, and as hard as it was to understand at the time, they trusted in him.

When a family hears a diagnosis for their child, they need the support of their church—from Christ followers who believe that every person is made in the image of God, that God created each person on purpose with a plan for his or her life, and that everyone has value regardless of the person's ability level. Not every doctor they talk to will believe that's true.

The message parents often receive from doctors or clinicians isn't a hopeful one. That's why we need to be prepared to join a family in the waiting room of the pediatric intensive care unit after they hear a diagnosis for their newborn, answer the call when we know a family has taken their toddler in for an evaluation, and respond to the text from the mom who says, "This wasn't in the adoption paperwork, and I don't know what to do." In those early days, after receiving a diagnosis and feeling like their lives are taking a turn they didn't expect, parents need their church families to show up. They need an anchor to steady them when it's all crashing down around them.

You don't have to have all the answers (or any answers!). What's most important is that you show up and sit with them. They need your presence and a promise that your church will keep showing up as they face an unknown future. Help them trust in God's goodness, even when what they're experiencing doesn't feel good. The family you're sitting with won't be more comforted by any cliché phrase you could come up with. They need to hear a prayer like Jehoshaphat's as he prepared his people for an attack: "We do not know what to do, but our eyes are on you" (2 Chron. 20:12).

As you communicate with the family, follow the biblical example of Elizabeth when she greeted Mary, who certainly got some plan-B news when she was told she would become pregnant with the long-awaited Savior of the world. Elizabeth told Mary that she was blessed and the child who would be born to her was blessed because Mary believed in the promises of the Lord (Luke 1:42–45). A special-needs diagnosis may not feel like a blessing in the early days, but being reminded of God's promises is a blessing that parents can hold on to. In the days and months after a family receives a diagnosis, put a reminder on your calendar to check in and keep checking in, even if the family doesn't respond. And be a soft place to land when they are ready.

Phase 2: Recover and Rebuild Rhythms

After James's autism diagnosis, it felt like everything changed for us. That included our school plans, the doctors we visited, having therapists over every day, diet changes and supplements, adding safety features to our home, and relationships with family members and friends. Our church even had to change, developing accommodations for James and launching a disability ministry so families like ours would be welcome. Those changes were hard to adjust to in those early days.

When a family is adjusting to life after a diagnosis, every member needs help meeting practical needs as they navigate all the changes a diagnosis can bring. And many families get into a new rhythm, and then that rhythm changes again when a family member has a long hospital stay, a parent is out of town for the weekend, or it's summer break for their kids who love the routine of the school year. Amy Moore, disability ministry director at Fellowship Bible Church in central Arkansas, shared that she was surprised by how hard it can be to get in touch with special-needs parents, especially when they are in this stage. They may not respond quickly to texts or emails. They may forget to respond at all. Don't take that personally. Keep reaching out and offering support.

What's important to remind families of at this stage is that *God cares about the details of our lives and the routines in our families.* One of my favorite stories of Jesus comes after his resurrection when he made breakfast for his disciples in John 21: "When they got out on land, they saw a charcoal fire in place, with fish laid out on it, and bread. Jesus said to them, 'Bring some of the fish that you have just caught. . . . Come and have breakfast'" (21:9–10, 12). I'm amazed by his care for the disciples after they had quite the plan-B experience! Even though he told them he would be killed and then be resurrected and return to them, how could they grasp what that meant? Especially on little sleep and empty stomachs. They wanted to return to what was comfortable and expected—their jobs as fishermen—but Jesus had so much more planned for them. And that plan started with breakfast. Jesus provided for their physical needs before he expected them to take the next steps with him.

I recently talked to the mom of two young men, the younger of whom has autism and other challenges similar to my son James's. We chatted about how she passes down her faith to her boys and how the church helps disciple them. She shared that they experienced a season of crisis in their home when all they could manage was having food available, keeping clean clothes accessible, and making it to school on time. There weren't family dinners around the table with Dad opening the Bible and Mom leading them in prayer. They couldn't think about meeting their spiritual needs until they could meet their physical needs. And during this season, their church stepped in to provide for their needs and support them by helping meet those practical needs.

So how does a church help in this phase of recovering and rebuilding rhythms? They look to the example of Jesus, who offered breakfast. They follow the pattern set by the early church in Acts and share with all in need (Acts 2:45). And they follow the admonitions from Paul in the book of Romans, "Contribute to the needs of the saints and seek to show hospitality" (12:13). Self-care can meet only so many needs. Verse after verse, example after example in the Bible show that we were created with a need for community care as well.

Family Care Plans

One way I recommend organizing the practical care these families will need is by creating family care plans. A family care plan is an info sheet kept by the staff to help know the family and how to care for their needs. Instead of having to ask a bunch of questions when a family is in crisis, you already have the information you need. You can create the plan when a family joins the church if you know it will be a part of the disability ministry or when a family who is part of your church gets a diagnosis. Anyone on staff who knows the family can go over the information with them. Once it's on file, the staff, small group, ministry leaders, or those who are part of your mercy ministries program can access it. Essentially anyone who would be organizing care for the family can first look at the family care plan to make it easier to provide the care they will need.

Here's what to include:

- names and ages of family members
- contact info
- classes or small groups the family members attend
- how they serve (so ministry leaders can get coverage when they aren't going to be at church)
- school(s) they attend
- diagnoses, medical concerns, allergies
- the family's chosen go-to person, who will step in to organize help when needed and who will communicate with the staff

The process for creating the plan also includes communicating with the family what the church offers as practical help and how the family can access that help. At our church, that includes who we recommend for counseling, respite opportunities, help with bills, meal train access, carpool opportunities, support groups through our church and other local churches, and advocacy agencies in the community.

> Even if you don't create family care plans, being aware
> of the practical needs of special-needs families and having
> ways to meet their needs will be a blessing to them.

Phase 3: Reinforce Your Faith Foundation

Because I had grown up as a special-needs sibling, there were many things about being a special-needs mom that weren't new to me. But one surprise I encountered was how it affected my relationship with God. I had unknowingly bought into prosperity-gospel beliefs, like if I followed all the rules and made God happy, he would reward me with healthy kids and an easy life. Didn't he owe me that much since I already had a sister with disabilities who would someday live with me and be my responsibility to care for?

In the months after James's diagnosis, I had to work through that erroneous belief and tear down the idol of control that I had been serving. I searched the Scriptures for stories I could relate to. I found one in Mark 9. A desperate father approaches Jesus to ask for healing for his son, who could not speak and had seizures (brought on by demon possession). The father brings his son to Jesus and asks, "If you can do anything, have compassion on us and help us." Jesus answers, "'If you can'! All things are possible for one who believes." The father responds, "I believe; help my unbelief!" (9:22–24). Like this father, I believed, but I still struggled with unbelief. I needed my church to support me as I built back a foundation of faith that would withstand the storms and suffering we faced as a family.

In phase 3, special-needs parents figure out what beliefs they may have held before that aren't actually true. Maybe they've believed they're being punished by God. Maybe this season reveals the idols they were putting their faith in. Maybe they had unknowingly bought into a prosperity-gospel message, believing that if they did everything right, God would bless them with healthy kids, and now they are rethinking everything since life didn't go according to their plan. They have to evaluate what they believed to find out the actual truth that will be powerful enough to get them through life as caregivers. In this season, parents need three things: They need a theology of disability based on Scripture, they need grace as they rebuild their trust in God and his goodness, and they need solid, biblical resources.

We explored Bible verses that are foundational for a theology of disability in chapter 1. You can talk through these verses with families and help them apply them to their lives as they rebuild their trust in God. As we help families who are confused by what God is doing in their lives and may be asking questions they've never asked before, let's remind them of what they know is true no matter how they feel.

As we help them strengthen their trust in God, let's do so with kindness and patience. When I'm suffering, nothing is more annoying than getting "chin up!" advice from someone who comes across as never suffering a day in life. What *does* help is compassion and empathy from those who have seen God faithful through their own struggles. Job 6:14 says, "A despairing man should receive loyalty from his friends / even if he abandons the fear of the Almighty" (CSB). This loyalty can bolster and strengthen struggling friends until they come through the fire and remember that not only were their friends standing with them, but so was their Savior.

Another important way to encourage families in this phase is to point them to biblical resources. Give them books by trusted authors who are raising kids with disabilities. (Our church often does this for Mother's Day and Father's Day.) Send them articles from your favorite websites that would encourage them. Recommend a podcast episode that would help them not feel alone. There are many solid, gospel-focused resources that will be a lifeline for them during this season.

Phase 4: Renew Relationships

In this phase, special-needs parents are ready to look around to see who is still standing beside them. They have the energy to invest in relationships because they have accepted plan B, established good routines in their homes, and have a renewed faith in God. Now they want to nurture their relationships with their spouses, typical kids, extended family members, and friends. The church has the opportunity to come alongside these families and help strengthen their relationships and support systems as they work through their needs during this phase. But there are a few possibilities to keep in mind as you help.

First, they have likely been hurt by family members or friends and need to learn to trust again. Any grief counselor will tell you that you'll be surprised by who does show up and who doesn't show up in hard times. I can remember exactly who surprised me by their presence and generosity in our lives (and I try to be understanding of those who pulled away or disappeared completely). Those reactions to our family influence how I make friends even now. Can I trust them to show up? Will we be too much for them? Will they treat James with kindness or indifference?

And these questions aren't just asked of friends—we can struggle in our relationships with extended family members as well. There's a family I know whose typical kids receive Christmas gifts from their grandparents each year, but their son with disabilities is left out because "he doesn't even know it is Christmas." He may not. But his parents and siblings do, and how the grandparents treat him affects their relationship with everyone in the family. We can help parents work through forgiveness and trust as they reconnect with family and friends and make new friends.

Second, they need support to strengthen their marriages and relationships with the typical children in their families. Most parents of a child with disabilities have seen pretty scary statistics about their increased chances of divorce. Fortunately, there hasn't been a good study to back up these scary stats. But they can certainly feel true when parents carry a heavier stress load while many of them face being caregivers for decades to come. Parents can also feel overwhelmed by all the ways they feel like they are failing their typical kids—there's just not enough time and energy to meet everyone's needs, and the most important needs (such as for safety) get met first, leaving little time for long conversations or fun family experiences. Churches can help families by offering respite events so parents can have a date night or recommend a trusted counselor who can help the couple strengthen their relationship.

Based on my experiences as a sister, there are also lots of ways churches can support typical siblings! Children's ministry and youth ministry leaders can take time to get to know each sibling as individuals (and avoid referring to them only as their sibling status, like "Syble's sister" or "James's brother"). They can help the siblings understand that God created them with unique gifts too (siblings often hear how special their brother or sister is, and being typical can feel like being unimportant). And they can teach them God has a plan for their lives, and that his plan includes using all their struggles and strengths. I'm so thankful for the influence my church family had on me as I was growing up, and I'm thankful for the ways our current church family has invested in and encouraged our older son. They fill in the gaps when my husband, Lee, and I just can't make everything fit.

Third, family members need opportunities to build relationships with others in similar situations. Hopefully you are encouraging parents to meet other parents of children with disabilities and providing time for them to talk. That could be casual conversations in the hall before they pick up their kids from the sensory room, or it could be through a support group or a small group just for parents of kids with disabilities. The best way to know how to support parents in building these relationships is to ask what would be most helpful. And if you can't provide the support they need, there are many online support groups that they can join to find friendship. See accessible-church.com for an up-to-date list of recommendations.

Phase 5: Reach Out to Others

In my book *Unexpected Blessings*, readers follow the story of Paul in Acts 27–28 as he ventures to Rome. During the voyage, Paul and his shipmates wreck onto the shores of Malta. I tell parents their journeys may feel a lot like Paul's. They will survive what feels like a shipwreck, and they will find themselves in a place they didn't expect but with the purpose God had for them all along. It wasn't an accident that Paul ends up on Malta. God had a purpose for his being there. Paul makes friends with the locals and performs miracles, blessing the families around him. When special-needs parents have moved through all the phases, they are ready to see who needs help. Like Paul, they are called to bless the families around them.

As a ministry leader, here's what you need to know about parents in phase 5. They are ready to serve! When they are in a good routine at home and feel supported at church, they are ready to plug in and use their spiritual gifts to build up the body. They may also have strong opinions about your ministry. These families have been advocating for their children in schools and with medical professionals. They believe they know best. What they don't always remember is the limitations we have at church and the goals we have are different from those in other environments. We can validate their concerns and respect their advice while also reminding them of what we can offer at church. Above all, they need to know that we value them and what they offer and that we want to empower them to do what they feel God is calling them to do. We want them to encourage others with the encouragement they have received and point people to the hope they have in Christ!

One of my favorite ways to encourage special-needs parents is to tell them they are missionaries. We know special-needs families are less likely to attend church than typical families. But missionaries don't wait for the lost to come to them. They are on mission wherever they go—the therapy waiting room, the support group, the hospital. The best way to grow your ministry and reach families with the message of the gospel is to empower your families to be on mission wherever they go!

Whole-Family Ministry

Disability ministry is truly whole-family ministry. The church I grew up in lived out this truth; as a result, of the several special-needs families that were there at the time, there are now four of us typical siblings in full-time ministry: a children's ministry director, a church planter, a music minister, and me. We grew up to love not only Christ but also his bride, the church. I want that to be true of the families your church serves as well. Let's take 1 John 3:18 to heart: "Little children, let us not love in word or talk but in deed and in truth" so that generations of special-needs families will know the love of Christ through the love of their church family.

Bringing It All Together

Based on what you learned in this chapter, here are steps of accessibility you can take:

Start by interviewing families in your church one on one to get to know them better and share the steps your church has taken so they can participate more.

Then try identifying what phase individual families in your church are in and what their needs are in that phase.

Next, apply what you've learned by creating family care plans for the special-needs families in your congregation.

7

Beyond Children's Ministry

Inclusion for Every Age and Life Stage

IN FEBRUARY, my sister Sarah and her teenage daughter Jayme volunteered at a church in Denver, Colorado, for the Tim Tebow Foundation's Night to Shine prom event. After the death of our big sister in 2022, Sarah and her family have been eager for ways to serve the disability community and their families. Night to Shine is a perfect fit. More than seven hundred churches host Night to Shine events in fifty-five different countries. Teens and adults with disabilities are kings and queens for the evening. They get to walk the red carpet as they enter, enjoy a meal with friends and volunteers, and dance the night away. Our sister loved to dance, so it was extra fun for Sarah and Jayme to join the kings and queens on the dance floor. It was a night of fun and joy for everyone who attended!

In the early years of churches hosting Night to Shine proms, the Tim Tebow Foundation received occasional feedback from families about a challenge they faced after the events. Some of the churches that celebrated them for that one big night weren't prepared to welcome them on a Sunday morning. Families felt more like projects than people worth forming ongoing relationships with to build up the church family. The Tebow Foundation responded quickly to this feedback by partnering with parachurch organizations that help equip churches and encourage families. These Shine On partners offer training resources for host churches so they feel ready for full inclusion. Now, Night to Shine kings and queens have the opportunity to be brothers and sisters in the churches that celebrate their gifts week after week.

As we shift from focusing on children's ministry to youth ministry and adult ministry, the methods and practices will change. The goal is the same—the gospel—but we want to shift our focus from doing ministry *to people* with disabilities to doing ministry *alongside people* with disabilities. As Joni Eareckson Tada writes, "As much as possible, a handicapped person should have the opportunity to get involved with able-bodied people, to share, to worship with them. Sitting side-by-side in pews, their voices can unite in praise."[1]

We want the same for teens and adults with disabilities as we want for all of our teens and adults: that they would grow in Christlikeness, have opportunities for friendship and fellowship, and build up the church with their gifts. Making sure this happens can take extra effort and creativity, but it is worth it.

In this chapter, let's look at what it means to be a church member as a teen and an adult with disabilities. How do we shift

---

1   Joni Eareckson Tada, *Barrier-Free Friendships: Bridging the Distance between You and Friends with Disabilities* (Grand Rapids, MI: Zondervan, 1997), 101.

from them *receiving* ministry to *participating in* ministry? We'll talk about setting up environments in which they can continue to flourish and grow. We'll also talk about opportunities for service in our churches as we remember our friends with disabilities are indispensable parts of the church body. Our ministries can expand with outreaches, weekday programs, and community partnerships. I'll share stories of churches doing this well from across the country. We'll also cover how to care for parents of adult children with disabilities who will be lifelong caregivers and may never have a true empty nest.

With a record number of young adults with developmental disabilities graduating from school and still needing care, let's make sure our inclusive ministries don't stop with their transition out of children's ministry or their graduation from high school. As my friend Garett Wall from Southeast Christian in Louisville, Kentucky, says, "Our participants aren't aging out of our ministry. We are caring for many of them from diagnosis to death." Our churches can be ready to support these families well.

Avoiding Childishness

A big challenge in this new stage of ministry is avoiding childishness with teens and adults. Anthony Emerson, the spiritual director at The Brookwood Community outside of Houston (which is a "God-centered nonprofit residential and vocational community for adults with disabilities"),[2] speaks of the differences between *childishness* and *childlikeness*. He reminds us, "They are

---

2   Welcome page on the Brookwood Community website, https://www.brookwood community.org/.

not children in adult bodies." But the childlikeness that we often see in teens and adults with intellectual disabilities is a strength when it comes to their faith and an example to our faith as well! In Matthew 18, Jesus used children as an example to the quarreling disciples:

> At that time the disciples came to Jesus, saying, "Who is the greatest in the kingdom of heaven?" And calling to him a child, he put him in the midst of them and said, "Truly, I say to you, unless you turn and become like children, you will never enter the kingdom of heaven. Whoever humbles himself like this child is the greatest in the kingdom of heaven." (18:1–4).

Emerson goes on to say, "Adults with intellectual disabilities don't need to become more like us. We all need to become more like children."

For this chapter, I interviewed ten ministry leaders who offer ministry opportunities for adults with disabilities, and their number one advice was to treat these adults as adults and not as children.[3] Jeff McNair of Trinity Evangelical Free Church in Redlands, California, says,

---

3 Here's a list of their names and the churches or organizations where they served at the time of the interview: Gary Felton of First Baptist Church Dallas, Texas; Meaghan Wall of Stonebriar Community Church in Frisco, Texas; Karen Roberts of First Presbyterian Church (EPC) of Aurora, Illinois; Beth Golik of Bay Presbyterian near Cleveland, Ohio; Jeff McNair of Trinity Evangelical Free Church in Redlands, California; Garett Wall of Southeast Christian Church in Louisville, Kentucky; Megan Petty of Compassion New England in Massachusetts; Shannon Pugh of Irving Bible Church in Irving, Texas; Anthony Palmiotto from Together We Care in Georgia; and Carley Ellis of Brentwood Baptist Church in Brentwood, Tennessee.

Adults should be treated as adults. If something is not happening in the other adult ministries, it should not be happening in our adult ministry. So [we do] adult songs, adult activities, and [focus on] adult topics for Bible lessons. The lessons we teach would be applicable for any adult who would attend.

Doing ministry alongside people with disabilities helps us to recognize the lessons we learn from them. They can model for the entire congregation characteristics that the Bible praises. Sevrin Hamilton, Program Manager at Guidelight, reminds us,

Perhaps those who navigate disability are more adept, seasoned veterans on the road to discipleship than we realize. As we grow in God's grace, the marks of our maturity are not our IQs or our pedigrees, our prowess, our milestones, or our monuments. It is rather humbly growing deeper in love with God and in service to our neighbor.[4]

When I spoke at my sister's funeral, I encouraged those in attendance to be more like her by trusting in the God of abundance to supply her needs and trusting in those around her to help meet those needs. If she needed extra time to get ready, extra ketchup with her fries, or extra cherries in her Shirley Temples, she just asked. She didn't pretend to be without needs. She couldn't pretend. And that's a helpful example for all of us.

---

4 Sevrin Hamilton, "DATC2023—Sevrin Hamilton—Discipleship and Disability: Growing in Grace Is for All God's Children," Key Ministry, May 9, 2023, YouTube video, https://www.youtube.com/. This session was given at Key Ministry's Disability and the Church Conference, 2023.

From "Ministry To" to "Ministry With"

Erik Carter describes the evolution of disability ministry as moving in this direction: *ministry apart, ministry to, ministry among, ministry with*, and finally *ministry by and with* people with intellectual disabilities. The evolution happened through the influence of special-education practices that started fifty years ago with the Education of All Handicapped Children Act, which declared that school-aged students with disabilities have the right to receive what Congress called a "free appropriate public education." My sister, born in 1977, benefitted from this act and was able to attend the same schools I attended. But her classes were often apart from my classes, with little interaction between those with developmental disabilities and the rest of us. Churches followed this model as well and faced similar challenges. But through the decades since, school, churches, and other organizations have seen the benefits of inclusion and integration. As Lamar Hardwick writes, "If we are going to set the right culture for disability-inclusive churches, we must understand that there is an enormous difference between being invited and being included."[5]

In Carter's work, he asked adults with disabilities what helped them feel like they belonged. He writes, "Although every person had a unique story to share, 10 dimensions of belonging emerged from across these numerous conversations." Dr. Carter and his team found that the keys to a sense of belonging included the people with disabilities feeling "*present, invited, welcomed, known, accepted, supported, cared for, befriended, needed*, and

---

5   Lamar Hardwick, *Disability and the Church: A Vision for Diversity and Inclusion* (InterVarsity Press, 2021), 51.

loved."[6] It might be helpful to think through this list and ask if these aspects of belonging are felt by the teens and adults in your ministry. Are there opportunities for growth? I think we can all say yes!

Now that we understand the shift that happens as our ministry participants become teens and adults and what they want through their inclusion in our church families, let's talk about the discipleship and service opportunities we can create to meet their needs and benefit from their strengths.

Options for Teens

Reverse Inclusion

As our son aged out of children's ministry, we needed to create a class that met our number one goal (communicating the gospel) but continued to provide the safety and structure that he needed. What works for us is a reverse-inclusion class. Reverse inclusion is a class designed for teens and young adults with disabilities. We invite typical teenagers and young adults into the class to build friendships.[7] It is similar to our public school's Peer Assistance and Leadership (PAL) program.[8]

The class, called the RISE class at our church (Reverse Inclusion Serves Everyone), enjoy activities that meet their interests in a sensory-friendly classroom. The RISE class is a natural next step for

6 Erik W. Carter, "A Place of Belonging: Including Individuals with Significant Disabilities in Faith Communities." *Inclusive Practices* 1, no. 1, 2022, 6–12, https://doi .org/10.1177/2732474520977482.

7 Content in this paragraph is adapted from Sandra Peoples, "Reverse Inclusion: Our Teen and Young Adult Class: Podcast Episode 078," Key Ministry, December 7, 2023, http://keyministry.org.

8 See the PAL US website: https://palusa.org.

the kids in a specialized ministry environment like a sensory class. We tried to make it look more like a teen room with a futon couch and a TV with a Nintendo Switch they can play. But it also meets their sensory needs and interests by including an indoor trampoline and a train table. You can customize it for the teens and adults who attend. The class meets in a building with other adult classes and is near our bathroom that has a universal-sized changing table and a shower if needed. There are also handicapped parking spaces in front of the building and a covered drop-off and pick-up area for rainy days.

Typical teens can apply to be part of the class with a recommendation from their youth pastor or an adult at church who knows them well. They can watch a training video on their role in the class and the goals of the class and let the ministry leader know whether they have any questions. They won't need the full buddy training that's needed for teens who serve in the preschool and elementary classes, but they can certainly do both. They can sign up to join the class once a month or more often. You can decide on additional policies or training that would work for your church and the students you have in the class.

Support in the Typical Youth Ministry Environment

Ryan Faulk from Joni and Friends shares, "The good news is that every church regardless of size, age, budget, or style is capable of doing effective ministry to students living with disability. It's about smoothing the path to make the ministry you already do accessible."[9] For the kids who are supported by buddies in our in-

---

9   Ryan Faulk, "Transitioning between Children's Ministry and Youth Ministry with Ryan Faulk and Joni & Friends," Vimeo, June 29, 2023, https://vimeo.com/84090 3200. This session was held at the All Access Disability Ministry Conference, 2022.

clusive children's ministry classes, we meet with parents and decide whether the RISE class or the typical youth group is a better fit for them. If the youth group is better for a student, that student continues to get help from a buddy (we use only adult buddies in youth ministry). The buddy is there to help facilitate connections and support positive behavior choices, but the hope is the buddy will largely be invisible to the student receiving help and his or her peers. Our goal is for the buddy to fade their support as the teen acclimates to the new ministry setting and matures. A lot of what we learned in the chapters on inclusion in children's ministry can apply to teens and young adults with disabilities, but it's important to avoid childishness in our lessons and interactions, to help them feel like they belong, and to have environments where their discipleship and fellowship needs can be met.

Bryan Barrineau is the lead student pastor at First Baptist Church in Enterprise, Alabama. He's been a youth pastor for more than twenty years and has seen an increase in the number of students who are neurodiverse or have other disabilities. Over 15 percent of the students currently in his ministry have a disability (including learning disabilities and behavioral diagnoses like ADHD). He did a helpful interview on the Youth Pastor Theologian podcast, on which the host, Mike McGarry, asked him questions like "How can youth workers better care for students with special needs, especially regarding youth with mild/moderate disabilities? And, within the dynamics of regular youth group programming, how do you encourage students to welcome struggling learners? What are some basic modifications we can make? His answers included suggesting that every couple of years they should do some type of teaching series about diversity and the kingdom of God and include disabilities as an expression of diversity. He also said that at the back of the room where they meet as a big group, they have a seating area for students with autism and ADHD to relax when they become overstimulated.[10]

The teen years are challenging for everyone, but especially for students who are also navigating a diagnosis and learning how to advocate for themselves. If you train leaders to be sensitive to their needs, educate peers on how to be kind and inclusive, and keep good communication with these students' parents to keep everyone in the loop on how each one is adjusting to the youth group environment, you can make your youth ministry a safe place for these students.

Ministry Environments for Adults

I mentioned that for this chapter I interviewed ten ministry leaders who support adults with intellectual and developmental disabilities in their ministries. They serve in churches of various sizes from California to Massachusetts and from Illinois to Georgia. Most of them hold staff positions at their churches. I asked detailed questions about class sizes and volunteer-to-participant ratios, how they supported caregiving parents, and whether they offered activities or opportunities beyond Sunday mornings. Here's what I learned!

First, let's consider the details about the classes they offer on Sunday mornings. These leaders serve a variety of ages, from eighteen-year-olds to participants in their seventies. Gary Felton of First Baptist Church in Dallas had recently led the funeral

---

10   Bryan Barrineau, "Serving Youth with Special Needs," *Youth Pastor Theologian Podcast*, episode 27, February 14, 2023, https://www.youthpastortheologian.com/.

service for one of the adults in his ministry, and the group spoke of supporting some of the same participants and their families for decades. The teacher-to-participant ratio varied and was based on the needs of those who regularly attended. One had a ratio of three teachers to eight to ten participants, and another came close to a one-to-one ratio. Some of the churches used curriculum designed specifically for adults with intellectual disabilities, like Bethesda, Lifeway's Access, With Ministries, Light & Power, Awe and Wonder, and Ability Ministry. Others adapted the curriculum the other classes in the church use. Carley Ellis from Brentwood Baptist in Brentwood, Tennessee, said they adapt the Gospel Project's preteen curriculum for their adult class.

I also asked whether the ministry participants attended the Sunday service, and if so, whether they sat together as a group or with their families. Their answers to these questions also varied. Many participants attend the service and sit with their families. Some sit together in a section where they are close to a door if they need to exit at any point. Felton said their group sits in a section in the balcony that is close to a lobby area with couches. At some churches, the adult class watched the service on a TV in their classroom. And at Southeast Christian, probably the biggest ministry represented in the group I interviewed, adult participants with disabilities have their own service together.

As we learned earlier from Erik Carter's work, it's important for people with disabilities to have opportunities to do ministry and not just be the recipients of ministry. I asked these ten ministry leaders how adults with disabilities were regularly serving in their churches, and I received many creative answers. At these churches—as well as in my own church—adults with intellectual disabilities serve in the greeter ministry, in preschool and children's ministries, and on tech teams. At Karen Roberts's church, they serve on the praise team and help lead worship. Others care for gardens on the church's property, help prepare the sanctuary for the worship service, and help with hospitality at special events. Anthony Palmiotto of Together We Care shared that at a church he and his wife, Jillian, served, one of the adults had always wanted to do voice-over work. When the children's ministry needed voices for their puppets, this man practiced and practiced so they could record his voice to use! Ministry participants also helped with special projects like Operation Christmas Child shoeboxes, craft projects, and running the church's cafe on Sundays.

All these ideas make it clear that adults with disabilities don't need to sit on the bench when it comes to serving just because they may need help to use their gifts to build up the church. Through a friend who worked with SOAR Special Needs Ministry, I heard of a church that took very seriously the call to include everyone in serving. One of the church's ministry leaders went to the leader of every service opportunity and asked, "What would it take for one of the adults in our disability ministry to be able to serve in your ministry area?" What would it take to help one of them be a greeter, or volunteer at vacation Bible school, or sing in the choir, or assist with a baptism? That ministry leader took the suggestions back to the disability ministry participants and let them sign up for what they wanted to do while also matching them with people who could help them fulfill their chosen role. What a great example of all the parts of a body working together!

Beyond Sunday Morning

After hearing about churches' Sunday morning experiences, I wanted to ask about opportunities throughout the week. Many of these churches offer a weekly Bible study for adults. Shannon Pugh of Irving Bible Church in Irving, Texas, said they have a larger number of participants for their weekday Bible study than they do on Sundays. And although their church doesn't host a day program, they do offer space to an organization that runs a day program at their church building. Megan Petty said one of her church's values is to be bigger on Mondays than they are on Sundays. Her church has multiple nonprofits—like a cafe and bookstore, food truck, and a resale shop—that fund the day program at her church.

The ministry leaders also talked about outreaches and extra opportunities. The Tim Tebow Foundation's Night to Shine prom event that I mentioned earlier is a popular choice. Beth Golik from Key Ministry shared three reasons she loves when her church outside of Cleveland hosts Night to Shine. First, "It brings the congregation and the community together in ways [she's] rarely seen happen with other events." Second, "Every *guest* is celebrated with a red-carpet experience. But the *parents and caregivers of the guests* are also invited to relax and be pampered with their own concurrent event." And third, it's a worldwide movement! More than seven hundred churches host Night to Shine events in fifty-five different countries.[11]

In addition to Night to Shine, churches put on other events to target teens and adults with disabilities. Meaghan Wall's church

---

11 Beth Golik, "My Three Favorite Things about Night to Shine," *Key Ministry: The Podcast*, episode 87, https://www.keyministry.org/.

rents out a water park and invites families to come. Other churches offer similar outreaches in their communities. In the Dallas, Texas area, so many churches do outreaches and events that the churches share details about the events with each other so families from every church have the opportunity to join them. Many churches also provide vacation Bible school and camp experiences. Our church offers a vacation Bible school specifically for children and adults with disabilities, doing it on Wednesday mornings each week in July. Garett Wall said one of his favorite experiences is taking close to two hundred people to camp for three days. Hearing about all the possible activities and the fun that these ministry leaders are having made me want to visit all their churches and join in!

Caring for Caregiving Parents

My sister lived with my parents until her passing in 2022. And my son James will always live with us or at a care facility. So as we talk about adult ministry, I want to include how churches can care for caregiving parents who may never be empty nesters. I asked the ministry leaders how many of their participants lived with a family caregiver and how many may live elsewhere. The majority live at home, although a couple of the churches I talked to invite group-home residents to be part of their classes and activities.

Facilitating opportunities for connection for caregiving parents was important to all the ministry leaders. Meaghan Wall noticed that the parents of the adults in the disability class would hang out "just in case" they were needed. So her church started a Sunday school class at the same time for the parents. Tom and Julie Meekins facilitate a parents' support group at Thomas Road

Baptist Church in Lynchburg, Virginia. They meet six times a year for fellowship and encouragement. Gary Felton's church has had success with short-term Bible studies for parents that happen on Sunday nights along with other classes offered by the church. His church also hosts quarterly ministry luncheons after Sunday morning services so special-needs families can stay on campus for a lunch together. This works well for the families his church serves because many of them drive long distances to get to the downtown Dallas location. Parents of kids with disabilities of any age benefit from having time together, but it's also important that they spend time with typical families so those families can benefit from their experiences. They all have experienced suffering and have testimonies of finding God faithful in their circumstances. That's an encouraging message brothers and sisters at church can apply to their own lives.

The Church (and the Floor) That Hold Up Max

One of my favorite examples of church accessibility and inclusion was written by Emily Colson about her son Max for the Key Ministry blog when I was an editor for the site.[12] Emily writes about their experience, "Every time I walk through the doors of our church I remember the years we lived in isolation, and the five years of staying home on Sunday mornings when we could not find our place. Autism held us hostage. But it is not a bitter memory; it is the soil from which God grew a victory. When I cross that threshold now with Max, it feels like holy ground." Max serves his church as a greeter and on the "grunt crew" that

12 Emily Colson, "The Church and the Floor That Hold Up Max," Key Ministry, July 1, 2016, https://www.keyministry.org/.

cleans up after services—a perfect role for Max, whose special interest is vacuums. Max also enjoys the worship music, praising God with his whole body. Emily writes,

> Most Sundays Max bounces so hard that one would expect him to go right through the wooden platform floor, dunk tank style. But he won't. Some of the men at church noticed the same risk. They got together one day and reinforced the floor where Max dances. It was months before anyone told me what the men had done. There was no mention of cost or inconvenience; no suggestion that perhaps the sound booth should not be used as a 1960s GoGo booth. Instead, they just strengthened the floor.

What a beautiful picture of what it looks like for the body to include and support one of their members. One of the discussions around the term "special needs" is that the needs of a person with a disability aren't that special. The needs are universal. The way we meet those needs may be special, creative, or unique, but the need itself is one everyone shares. We can see that in Max's story.

Emily concludes the story from how her church supported Max: "Maybe this is what we all want—to find the spot where we belong, and to know that others will hold us up in it." Whether or not ministry to teens and adults with disabilities is high on your priority list or on your "someday it would be nice" list, I hope the discussion in this chapter about the aspects of belonging and the creativity of the ministry leaders you met will help expand your church's plans for accessibility to reach beyond children's ministry.

Bringing It All Together

Based on what you learned in this chapter, here are steps of accessibility you can take:

Start by assessing your church's current need for opportunities for teens and adults and the timeline for when the families you currently serve will need the next phase of support.

Then try launching a reverse inclusion class for teens and young adults.

Next, apply what you've learned by creating a list of service opportunities for teens and adults with disabilities.

Growing Your Ministry

Marketing and Outreach Ideas

MATTHEW 9 says when Jesus saw the crowds that were following him, "he had compassion for them, because they were harassed and helpless, like sheep without a shepherd. Then he said to his disciples, 'The harvest is plentiful, but the laborers are few; therefore pray earnestly to the Lord of the harvest to send out laborers into his harvest'" (9:36–38). If Jesus walked among us today, he would have compassion for special-needs families. The functional and social obstacles of disability often leave disability families feeling harassed and helpless. As his followers, we can be sent into his harvest to reach disability families and communicate the hope of the gospel with them.

Henry Blackaby summed up discerning the will of God by telling us to see where God is working and join him. I believe it's clear that God is working in the lives of people with disabilities and their families. I've been in accessible churches my entire life, and I've never been more optimistic about the opportunities for inclusion than I am right now. My prayer through my role as the disability ministry consultant at the Southern Baptists of Texas Convention is "Every church, every family." I want every church in our convention to be equipped to welcome every family.

Becoming accessible is the first step. Letting people know we are accessible is the next step. This is how we grow our ministries. When moving toward growing your ministry, there are two approaches to consider. The first is *come and see*. The second is *go and tell*. When Jesus communicates with his followers, first the message is *come and see*, then the instructions are *go and tell*. In our context, *come and see* will include how you communicate accessibility to families through your church website, social media, and within the congregation. *Go and tell* will include how we get the message of inclusion out to our communities. This includes outreach ideas, community partnerships, and equipping church members to be missionaries.

Come and See

Your Church Website

Most special-needs families are going to visit your church's website before they visit in person. Your church's goal is to be as prepared as possible for disability families when they come, to make their experience smooth for them and for your team. To make sure you're catching every family, you can give three options on the website for them to find out more about your church and for you to find out more about them: First, have a page for your disability ministry. Second, provide info about your options for inclusion on the children's ministry page. Third, include a question on your registration form that invites parents to give you more info about their children.[1]

First, on the main website: In the drop-down menu or list of ministries, you can list your special-needs or disability ministry as an option. On the page you create for your ministry, you can give information about the options your church provides, like buddies in the typical classes and what ages they are available for, and whether you have specialized classroom options for children, teens, and adults with more significant needs. You'll want to make clear how they can visit you for the first time. You can supply a contact form or contact information for a ministry leader, or you can make available a registration form they can fill out. If certain classes are offered only at specific times, make that clear.

It's important to use real pictures of the classrooms when possible to help decrease anxiety for those who are visiting. You'll want them to picture their kids in your ministry spaces. It can be especially helpful to have a welcome video on your website. You can start in the parking lot, show them what door to go through, and even take them into the classroom. Social stories are also a helpful idea. You can create one that families can download and share with their kids. (Find examples at accessible-church.com.)

In addition to having a page specifically for your disability ministry, you may want to include information on your children's ministry page in case that's where someone looks first, or if the family has a child with a behavior diagnosis or a learning disability. These kids benefit from steps of inclusion, but they don't always consider themselves to be part of the disability ministry. On the

---

[1] Content in this paragraph is adapted from Sandra Peoples, "Ministry Visibility on Your Church Website," Key Ministry, May 14, 2024, https://www.keyministry.org/.

children's ministry page, you could include a blurb about the buddies you have available to help kids and include a picture of what that looks like (getting permission from the families included) and give them a step to take if they want to learn more or a link to your disability ministry page.

If you are a multisite campus, make it clear on your website whether there are certain accessibility options available on only certain campuses, but don't put that info only on the page for that campus. For example, if your north campus has a specialized class in a sensory-friendly room, but the south campus offers buddies only in the typical classes, put that info on both pages. A family would likely be willing to drive further for the option their child needs, but if that information is only on the page for the north campus and they are looking at the page for the south campus, they won't realize they have the option.

There's a third way you can make sure you're as prepared as possible to welcome students with additional needs, and you can take this step for Sunday mornings and for activities like vacation Bible school or kid's camp. You can put a question on your registration form that invites parents of kids with any kind of need or diagnosis to be up-front and honest. I like to use language that covers as many concerns as possible, something like "We care about the safety and success of all the children in our ministry. To help us prepare, please let us know if your child has any allergies, learning disabilities, behavioral or mental health diagnoses, or other disabilities or special needs." Some churches ask a question like, "Does your child need an IEP or 504 plan to be successful at school?," which works well. Either way, you can follow up with the family for more info by using a detailed form or having a conversation.

10 Questions to Include on Your Intake Form

To get to know a new child visiting your church, it's helpful to get some basic information ahead of time to be prepared to support him or her. You can start with these ten questions:

1. Name and birthdate of child?
2. Parents' names and contact info?
3. Does your child have any allergies or medical conditions?
4. What is your child's primary diagnosis, and are there any related diagnoses?
5. What are your child's strengths?
6. What are the child's interests? What brings him or her joy?
7. What are some possible triggers for stress?
8. How is your child comforted in times of stress?
9. How does the child primarily communicate?
10. What are the child's toileting needs?

Communicating with Your Congregation

As we talked about in chapter 3, you are an advocate for families with the staff at your church. You are also an advocate for them with the congregation! Increasing accessibility can bring changes to the entire church. And it's helpful to educate everyone on why accessibility is important so families feel welcome, not only in the programs designed for them (like inclusive children's ministry classes) but also when they are in the services with the entire church family.

As you advocate for people with disabilities and their families with the congregation, you'll want to show respect and maintain their dignity. Dan Vander Plaats had developed the 5 Stages of Changing Attitudes with Elim Christian Services.[2] The first stage is *ignorance*. People don't know what they haven't experienced or been exposed to. By including people with disabilities in your church, your people will quickly move past ignorance. The second stage is *pity*. Many people in your congregation may currently have pity for people with disabilities. But we don't want them to stay there! They can move through the other stages: *care*, *friendship*, and *colaboring*. You can help church members move from one stage to the next as you educate and advocate.

This advocacy with the congregation happens during services, in conversations, and on social media. It can sound like the following examples:

- Our church includes many special-needs families. Here's how you can help them feel more welcome in a service or in your small group.
- In order to welcome as many kids as possible, we need volunteers to be buddies at vacation Bible school this year! Sign up to get trained to help!

2   Dan Vander Plaats, "The 5 Stages of Changing Attitudes," Wheaton Center for Faith and Disability, 2014, https://www.wheaton.edu/wheaton-center-for-faith-and-disability/.

- It's Autism Awareness Month! Did you know many people with autism don't feel welcome at church? Here's how we can all make sure they are welcome here.
- This week our friends with disabilities are serving our church family with the gifts God has given them! Let's thank them for serving as greeters.

One way we work toward advocacy and ministry visibility both at our church and through our state convention of churches is by having Disability Ministry Sunday each year. It's officially on our calendar for the second Sunday in July. We use Disability Ministry Sunday as an opportunity to "educate church members about the value of all people, a way to share more about how churches can make accommodations for those who need them, and as an outreach to special-needs families who are longing for a church home."[3]

Churches across our state celebrate Disability Ministry Sunday in ways that work best for their churches. At First Baptist Church in Forney, Texas, Pastor Nathan Lino preached a sermon entitled "God Deliberately Formed You in the Way That Would Bring Him Maximum Glory" from Exodus 4:10–12.[4] At Harmony Hill Baptist Church in Lufkin, Texas, ministry director Cynthia Pounds invited special-needs families to share their stories as part of the service. One year at our church we created calls to action for the children's ministry, youth ministry, and adult life groups. The teachers in each children's ministry class read books

3   "Disability Ministry Sunday," The Southern Baptists of Texas Convention, http://sb texas.com.
4   Nathan Lino, "Exodus 4:10–12," Vimeo, June 2, 2024, available at https://vimeo.com /channels/fbcforney/.

that encouraged inclusion, the youth group talked about how to be a good friend, and the adults were asked to pray, volunteer, and deepen friendships with people with disabilities. Disability Ministry Sunday is a helpful way to recognize the contributions of people with disabilities and their families and educate the church on their belonging as important members of the body!

Go and Tell

Outreach Events

Outreach events can be a really important part of what your church does to serve disability families in your community. Because our church considers disability families as an unreached or unchurched people group, we are on mission to reach them where they are. Before we discuss the actual outreach ideas, let's first consider their purpose. There are five purposes of outreach events that you can think through as you're planning the event ideas that you have.

The first purpose of outreach events is to bless the families that attend your church. We want special-needs families to be blessed and to be encouraged and to be supported in our church. So doing outreach events with the purpose of blessing those families is an important reason.

The next purpose is to reach new families. We do outreach events in the community or outside Sunday morning activities because we want to reach new families and introduce them to our church and let them know our church is a safe place for their kid with disabilities and also a safe place for the entire family.

The third purpose is to provide a service for the community. When you do an outreach event that's outside your church walls, that blesses your entire community! That's a way to let everyone know you care for families impacted by disabilities and the first step in sharing the gospel with them.

The fourth purpose is to foster relationships between special-needs families. There are many reasons they need to lean on others in challenging times, a truth they understand that people outside that circle may not. So providing opportunities for families to share with each other and talk to each other is an important reason to have an outreach event.

Then the last important reason is to share the gospel. That could be showing the love of Christ through our acceptance and our actions, and it could be actually sharing a gospel message. Even if the outreach event itself doesn't provide an opportunity to share the gospel, doing so can be part of your follow-up plan. Remember that this is the goal for all we do.

9 Questions to Ask When Planning an Outreach Event

1. What is the purpose of our event? We just looked at what the purposes could be, and this is the first question you want to answer when planning an event so you make sure you reach that goal.

2. What ages will we serve? Is this primarily a children's ministry, youth ministry, or adult ministry activity? Is it for multiple levels of participants?

Knowing the ages you will target will help you bring in the right team members to help.

3. Are we going to include just the person with a disability, the typical siblings, or the entire family in this event? Different events can include different family members.

4. What volunteer-to-participant ratio is doable? Do we need any specialized volunteers? Some events need a one-to-one ratio, one volunteer for each participant. But other events include the whole family, so only a few volunteers are needed. This is an important question to answer early in your planning so you can know how much recruiting to do.

5. How will they register? What is the deadline to register? Is there a cost to the families? These details need to be decided before you start marketing the event so everything is set up to be a smooth process for the family.

6. How will we advertise this event? There are lots of options for advertising: word of mouth from your church members, social media posts, asking your school district to help spread the word, through your community partnerships, through local Facebook groups parents are involved in, and more. As you decide how you will advertise, think about what you will need, like graphics or flyers.

7. What is your budget, and what supplies will you need? If you'll feed everyone or need supplies for projects, make sure you've made a budget and a plan for getting what you need ahead of time.

8. Can you use this outreach event as a training opportunity for those interested in volunteering in your ministry? In chapter 4, we discussed using respite and outreach events as ways to train those who may be interested in volunteering. Are you planning an event that would work well as a training event too?

9. How will you follow up with the families who attend? You don't want to hold an event and not connect with families again. Make sure there's a follow-up plan and you're capturing their information so you can follow up with them and continue to share whatever your church offers.

Since James was diagnosed with autism in 2010, we have been part of two churches and one church plant that all grew in accessibility. Through those experiences, we've tried lots of outreach ideas to reach and bless special-needs families. Some target just the kids or teens with disabilities, and some include the whole family. Some require a budget to cover expenses, and others can be done with relatively low costs. And since we held some of these events as a church plant that met in our living room, there are some events you can do even if you don't have a church building!

No matter what your goals and limitations are, you can find an outreach option that can work for your church.

The first one (and often the most popular idea) is a respite event. Respite nights are a great way to serve the families in your church and reach even more families in your community. We do respite nights four times a year, and so it's a low commitment for our volunteers, but we really have a great time when we do them.

What is a respite event? It's a few hours when parents can drop off their kids with disabilities so they get an opportunity to have a date night or go home and take a nap if that's what they want to do with their time. The kids can watch movies, do art projects, play games, and eat together. At our events, they take over the elementary and preschool halls and can play with whatever they want to. We have a craft room if they want to do crafts and a movie room if they want to watch a film. We include siblings who want to attend, and our volunteers can bring their entire families so kids in the volunteer families can play too.

There are organizations that can help your church plan and host a respite event, like 99 Balloons and Nathaniel's Hope. Ginney Mooney and I corresponded via email about how much her daughter Lena benefits from respite events. She writes,

> Most spaces that Lena enters, the people who love her have made these spaces to adapt to her. Even in our church community, when she comes on a Sunday morning to church, the church . . . is actually a lot of work for her because she is trying to use those modifications to settle and be a part. Whereas something like rEcess, or a specific respite program, is designed for her completely.

Additionally, 99 Balloons helps churches host "rEcess" respite events by providing training and activity ideas. Nathaniel's Hope also provides help for churches interested in providing "Buddy Break" respite events at their churches. In addition to these events, Nathaniel's Hope hosts Make 'Em Smile community events around the country. At Make 'Em Smile, people with disabilities are celebrated with activities designed for them to enjoy. Their recent event in Orlando, Florida, included three thousand "VIPs" along with their families and caregivers.

Jill's House, founded by the family of Lon Solomon when he pastored McLean Bible Church outside of Washington, DC, provides weekend respite at their facility. Their goal is also to provide an environment where kids and teens with disabilities can come as they are. They have expanded this concept by partnering with campgrounds to provide Weekend Adventures as a respite option for families. They partner with local churches to staff these programs. If you're interested in offering respite events, you can get help from one of these organizations and bless families in your church and community.

The next idea is a sensory-friendly movie event. Many special-needs families have never gone to the movies together because the sensory experience is too much for their member with a disability. But your church could help make that opportunity accessible for them. Your community may have a theater that you could rent out either before it is open to the public or in a room where it hosts birthday parties and other events. What makes the movie sensory friendly is that the lights are a little brighter and the sound is quieter. We also advertise the events as being sensory friendly so families know whether their child makes noise or needs to get up and down a couple of times—all the parents understand!

We have a privately owned theater in our small town, which lets us host movies there on Saturday mornings. Admission is free, but the families can buy what they want from the concessions. Before the movie starts, my husband, Lee (our pastor), welcomes the families, tells them what to expect, shares a gospel message, and gives the families an opportunity to pray with our members who are volunteering. Since we have the theater to ourselves, we also set up tables in the lobby with coloring sheets that go along with the movie for kids who need a break.

Sensory-friendly movies are a great option because they don't require a lot of volunteers. You can have greeters at the doors who capture names and email addresses for follow up and people to pray with families. But since families are together for the event, it doesn't require much work other than at the beginning. And it's lots of fun for the families!

Another event that we've had a lot of success with is a family photo session. It can be difficult for special-needs families to find a photographer who is patient with their kids and understanding of the challenges they face. If you know someone who takes great pictures and goes with the flow, you can plan an event either at your church with a photo backdrop you've set up or in a public location like a park. We've hosted this event at a park and picked a spot where there weren't many people. We brought benches and chairs to use. The families signed up for designated times, we took their pictures, and we sent them an email with the best options. It's especially helpful to do these in the late fall so families can use them for Christmas cards. Similarly, if your church has backdrops or photo booths for special days such as Mother's Day or Christmas, you could invite the special-needs families to come to the church when there aren't many people around so they can take pictures without feeling rushed or like they have an audience.

Next, try to think of various activities that families enjoy doing together that special-needs families may be less likely to do because they're afraid not everyone would be accepting of their differences. Then you can plan for a group of them to go together so they feel less alone. It could include going to a public pool or splash pad, going produce picking (like apples or strawberries), or visiting a pumpkin patch and corn maze. The special-needs families in your church and in your community can meet each other, have fun together, and let their guard down a little because everybody understands the quirks of being in a special-needs family.

The last idea I want to mention focuses on moms and female caregivers. It's a day of pampering. This is an outreach I got to participate in at a church that friends of mine attended, and it was so lovely. The church planned the event on a Saturday from ten in the morning till two in the afternoon. It started with the moms and caregivers getting valet parking from the men's ministry. While we attended the event, the men (with help from boys in the youth group) washed and detailed our cars. The day included singing together, hearing from a speaker, participating in a blessing of the hands, and enjoying lunch with women from the church who served as table hosts. Then they had people come in to provide haircuts, manicures, and facials. It was such a relaxing, enjoyable day and a great way to serve caregivers who often feel like their work is unseen and unappreciated by others. We can remind them that God sees them and cares for them, and so do our churches!

Community Partnerships

Community partnerships are another important way to spread the word about your church's accessibility. You can make connections with your school district, local therapy providers, disability-focused organizations like Special Olympics or the Arc, and local support groups. Our church has a good relationship with our school district, so when we do a respite event or other outreach, they include the details in their community newsletter. Our church in Pennsylvania hosted a monthly meeting for the county's autism support group when the school where they usually met was under construction. Those families were able to see the ways we made our classrooms accessible, and they knew they would be welcome back on a Sunday. Amy Moore from Fellowship Bible Church in Central Arkansas has made connections with service and therapy providers in her community. She takes treats by their offices and offers her church as a location for training events. Families often ask therapists and service providers for more resources in their communities, and when they do, your church could be the first place mentioned.

It's also helpful for the families in your church to be aware of opportunities in the community you could direct them to. My friend Sharonda Ausbie, a disability ministry volunteer at Champion Forest Baptist Church in Houston, helps organize a resource fair each year. The event connects families with community resources that can support them now or in the years to come as their children transition out of school. As we saw in chapter 7, Shannon Pugh at Irving Bible in Irving, Texas, hosts a day program at their church for adults with disabilities. These opportunities and partnerships can benefit everyone involved.

Members as Missionaries

The final way we want to invest in the go-and-tell approach is to equip church members to reach out to the special-needs families they know and invite them to church. Our members get excited when they can tell an extended family member or a neighbor, "Your family would be welcome at our church!" You could print out cards that include your disability ministry's website, or a QR code that links to it, and pass them out to church members who could give them to people they know. And as you read in chapter 6, you can also encourage special-needs parents to be on mission wherever they go—inviting other parents they meet in waiting rooms or at Special Olympics practice to come to their church or an outreach event. Equipping members as missionaries is a great way to grow your ministry.

Bringing It All Together

Based on what you learned in this chapter, here are steps of accessibility you can take:

Start by adding information about your inclusion options on your church's website.
Then try educating your congregation through family testimonies or a Disability Ministry Sunday.
Next, apply what you've learned by planning a respite night or outreach event.

Conclusion

ONE OF MY FAVORITE professors in seminary had a daughter with autism. He spoke of her often and about how being her dad had made such a difference in his life. I was pregnant with James during my last semester, so I didn't know until a few years later that I would also have a child with autism. But even as a sibling in a special-needs family, I felt a connection to how he had been changed by his daughter. One of his favorite stories from the life of Jesus that we often talked about was the healing of blind Bartimaeus. It is found in Matthew, Mark, and Luke. Let's look at Mark's account:

> And they came to Jericho. And as he was leaving Jericho with his disciples and a great crowd, Bartimaeus, a blind beggar, the son of Timaeus, was sitting by the roadside. And when he heard that it was Jesus of Nazareth, he began to cry out and say, "Jesus, Son of David, have mercy on me!" And many rebuked him, telling him to be silent. But he cried out all the more, "Son of David, have mercy on me!" And Jesus stopped and said, "Call him." And they called the blind man, saying

to him, "Take heart. Get up; he is calling you." And throwing off his cloak, he sprang up and came to Jesus. And Jesus said to him, "What do you want me to do for you?" And the blind man said to him, "Rabbi, let me recover my sight." And Jesus said to him, "Go your way; your faith has made you well." And immediately he recovered his sight and followed him on the way. (Mark 10:46–52)

When we read this encounter, we often focus on Jesus—and we should! We can also connect with Bartimaeus, who cries out to Jesus for help, is healed, and then joins Jesus's followers. But as we wrap up this book, I want to focus on the crowd. They experience their own transformation in this short account. It can be the same transformation our churches experience as well when we become accessible.

In verse 47, Bartimaeus cries out from his spot on the roadside. He hears Jesus is passing by, and he asks for mercy. Many in the crowd rebuke him, however, telling him to be silent (10:48). Some people with disabilities and their families feel that same silencing from a crowd. They feel pushed into the background, away from community and sometimes even away from Jesus. But then Jesus stops and calls Bartimaeus. The crowd then changes its reaction. Instead of rebuking Bartimaeus, the people understand that Jesus wants to meet this man and respond to his needs. So they say to Bartimaeus, "Take heart. Get up; he is calling you" (10:49). They extend the invitation from Jesus. They see that Bartimaeus has value in Jesus's eyes and should have value in their eyes as well. When Jesus asks Bartimaeus what he wants and Bartimaeus replies that he wants his sight, Jesus heals him.

In Luke's account, it is written, "And immediately he recovered his sight and followed him, glorifying God. And all the people, when they saw it, gave praise to God" (Luke 18:43). Bartimaeus joins the crowd following Jesus after his encounter with him. The crowd praises God for the work Jesus has done in Bartimaeus's life. First the crowd impedes Bartimaeus from getting close to Jesus, then they invite him to meet Jesus, and finally they include him as a follower of Jesus.

There may be families in your community who feel like they're impeded from getting to Jesus because they don't think church is accessible to them. They may have even been told as much by churches in the past. But you can go to them and invite them into fellowship with your church family. And together you can praise God for what he has done in their life and in the life of your church!

God is using his people to break down more barriers each and every day as families show up, churches welcome them, and denominations and curriculum writers provide resources to help. Because new resources get added so often, I've created a website to accompany this book that will be kept up to date. Visit accessible-church.com today to get resources that accompany this book and connect with others working toward inclusion.

Let's join the crowd following Jesus who includes blind Bartimaeus and give glory to God for his wonderful works!

Acknowledgments

ADDING THE WORDS of this book to the decades of work on the topic of church inclusion has been an honor, and there are many people I want to thank for giving me the opportunity and supporting me along the way.

The material for this book was first content for the Gospel Centered Family's Disability Ministry Cohort. Jared Kennedy asked me to lead that cohort and gave me the opportunity to invest in ministry leaders from across the country (and one international participant!). Believing in the importance of accessible churches, Jared introduced me to Champ Thornton at Crossway, who was a wonderful advocate through the process. Editor Kevin Emmert made the book stronger with his suggestions and feedback. I'm deeply thankful for the work of Champ, Kevin, and the entire Crossway team.

As I was writing, I got valuable feedback from friends and early readers. Thank you, Beth Golik of Key Ministry and Bay Presbyterian Church in Bay Village, Ohio; Amy Moore of Fellowship Bible Church in Little Rock, Arkansas; Dr. Chris Hulshof of Liberty University; Dr. Tracy McElhattan of Blue Valley Church in Overland Park, Kansas; and Stephanie Hubach of Covenant Theological Seminary in St. Louis, Missouri.

The disability ministry community feels like a family, and I'm thankful for the brothers and sisters who I have learned from in the last decade of being in this field. Many of them are mentioned throughout the book, but I want to specifically say thank you to Nicole Filak and Julie Hernandez, who have led the ministries at the churches where we were members in the years since James's diagnosis. Recently my work has focused on equipping children's ministry leaders and other church staff members with the tools they need to make their churches more welcoming for people with disabilities. Dr. Karen Kennemur has been a wise guide in this ministry area, as well as a helpful advocate through our work together at the Southern Baptists of Texas Convention and as my PhD advisor at Southwestern Baptist Theological Seminary.

Finally, I'm thankful for the support of friends and family who made this book possible through their practical help and made it better through their encouragement and feedback. My parents, Carl and Thresia; my husband, Lee; and my boys, David and James, all deserve to have their names listed as contributors. I am thankful for their investment in me and the mission of accessibility.

Discussion and Application Questions

IF YOU ARE USING this book as a textbook for a class or as a training resource, here are discussion questions and assignment ideas you can use or adapt.

Chapter 1: Laying the Foundation—A Theology of Disability

1. What is a challenge or limitation you have faced, and how has God been faithful as you've faced that challenge?

2. Choose a passage that was discussed in the chapter and dig deeper, using at least three sources that help you understand how the passage applies to your theology of disability. Summarize your observations with the group.

3. How does God's promise that we will spend eternity in perfect fellowship with him and each other bring you hope today?

Chapter 2: Who Is Missing? Do Our Pews Reflect Our Communities?

1. Define the functional and social aspects of disability and explain how they could affect a disabled person's church experience.

2. Did your previous understanding of special-needs ministry include the categories for disability that were discussed in this chapter? If not, how did this chapter expand that view?

3. Develop a disability ministry mission statement based on your theology of disability and the goals you would have for the ministry.

Chapter 3: Preparing for Accessibility— Programs, Places, and Policies

1. What is the goal of inclusion and accessibility in our churches?

2. List the four common options for accessible environments.

3. What policies at your church do you need to review and adjust for accessibility?

Chapter 4: Your Ministry Team— Everyone Has a Role in Accessibility

1. Based on your current church's size and resources, what roles would you put on your ministry team? Would they be paid or volunteer? How many volunteers would you need each week?

2. What characteristics would you look for in someone who would be a good disability ministry leader or volunteer? And why would those characteristics be important for people working with students with disabilities?

3. List the four steps to volunteer assimilation and share why each step is important.

Chapter 5: Student Support—The Goal Is the Gospel

1. What is your understanding of the concept of Universal Design for Learning? How have you seen it applied in a children's ministry classroom?

2. Think of a common activity at church and create a rubric of ISP goals for that activity (examples: lesson time, prayer, music).

3. List the ABCs of behavior and share why they are each important in understanding how to support positive behavior choices.

Chapter 6: Whole-Family Inclusion—Strengthening Marriages and Supporting Siblings

1. Describe how to support a family in your church who has received a diagnosis. Choose an at-birth diagnosis (such as Down syndrome or cerebral palsy), elementary-age diagnosis (such as autism level 1 or ADHD), or later-in-life diagnosis (such as dementia or paralysis) and indicate your choice/the diagnosis in your answer.

2. As churches offer options for friendship and connection to parents of children with disabilities, there are two options to consider: small groups with a mix of different types of families, and support groups specifically for caregiving parents. Compare the types of groups and the benefits and weaknesses of each type. What would you recommend a church offer?

3. Choose one of the five phases of special-needs parenting and create a list of at least three resources that would support a family in that stage.

Chapter 7: Beyond Children's Ministry— Inclusion for Every Age and Life Stage

1. Why is childlikeness a characteristic all believers should strive for?

2. Share your understanding of why it's important to shift to doing ministry alongside people with disabilities.

3. What recommendations would you give to a youth minister who wants to make his ministry more accessible?

Chapter 8: Growing Your Ministry— Marketing and Outreach Ideas

1. Research a parachurch organization in the field of disability ministry and share what resources they provide.

2. What changes can you make to your church's website to communicate your accessibility to families?

3. What are the benefits of a church offering a respite event for a disability family?

General Index

99 Balloons, 154, 155

Aaron, 78
accessible churches, 1–2
   and a model for belonging and
      accessibility for those with dis-
      abilities, 37–42
   and support for those with mental
      health conditions, 36
accessible environments, 48
   hybrid of inclusive and specialized
      options, 56–57
   inclusive environments, 48–49,
      48–53
   specialized environments, 54–55
activity
   nonpreferred activity, 51
   preferred activity, 51
ADHD, 34, 35, 36, 49, 133, 134
advocacy, 148–49
   with pastors and church staff, 73
Alzheimer's disease, 30
Angelman syndrome, 31
attachment disorders, 49
Ausbie, Sharonda, 158
autism, 31–32
   autism spectrum disorder (level 1),
      49.
   See also Peoples, James, autism of

Bartimaeus, 161–63
Beates, Michael, 7, 14, 28
Beeke, Joel, 9–10
behavior
   the ABCs of behavior, 102
   behavior challenges, 101–4
Bible and Disability, The (Melcher,
      Parsons, and Young), 7
bio sheets and buddy bag lanyards,
      99–100
Blackaby, Henry, 143–44
blindness, 31
Boehm, Thomas, 22–23

caregiving parents (caring for),
      138–39
Carter, Erik, 74, 130–31, 135
children
   communication with children who
      don't communicate with words,
      55–56
   safety policies and communication
      for children with disabilities, 57
classroom safety, 60–61, 63–64
   for high medical needs, 58–59
   security for eloping children,
      59–60
   toileting policies, 58
churches. *See* accessible churches

Scripture Index